The Shorter MBA

Barrie Pearson and
Neil Thomas

THOROGOOD

This edition published in Great Britain
in 2011 by Thorogood Publishing Ltd
10-12 Rivington Street
London EC2A 3DU
Telephone: 020 7749 4748
Fax: 020 7729 6110

Email: info@thorogoodpublishing.co.uk
Web: www.thorogoodpublishing.co.uk

Revised and updated in 2012

First published in Great Britain by
Thorsons, an imprint of
HarperCollins*Publishers*, 1991

© Barrie Pearson and Neil Thomas,
1991, 2004, 2012

A CIP catalogue record for this book is
available from the British Library.

ISBN 1 85418 787 2
     978 185418787 1

Book designed and typeset by Driftdesign

Printed and bound in Great Britain by
Marston Book Services Limited, Didcot

Contents

PART THREE
BUSINESS DEVELOPMENT

Introduction and acknowledgements

About the book

Authors and contributors

About the book

This book aims to provide a practical approach to effective business skills for personal and business success, with tips and techniques to help you achieve your goals. It is divided into three main parts:

- Personal development
- Management skills
- Business development

The structure and format are designed to help you to grasp the essential ingredients of:

- Personal success – of high achievement, time management, personal effectiveness, leadership, teambuilding, solving problems and decision-making, innovation, effective communication skills, mentoring/coaching and personal marketing and PR;

- Management success – through understanding finance, human resources management and competitive marketing strategy;

- Business success – through strategies for growth and preparing a business plan, through the buying and selling of unquoted companies, and through management buy-ins and buy-outs.

Barrie Pearson, Neil Thomas

Authors and contributors

Contributing editors

Barrie Pearson BSc, FCMA is chief executive of Realization, which delivers world class mentoring and coaching for chief executives and entrepreneurs, (email: realization@eidosnet.co.uk). In 1976, he founded Livingstone Guarantee, the first corporate finance boutique in the UK, and sold it for a substantial sum in 2001. Previously he had an international executive career with The De La Rue Company, The Plessey Company and Dexion Comino International. He co-wrote with Neil Thomas *Me-Time*, a life coaching manual, published by Thorogood.

Neil Thomas MA is chairman of Falconbury (www.falconbury.co.uk), a management training specialist (especially Mini-MBAs). He has worked with John Adair to produce *The Best of Adair on Leadership and Management, The Concise Adair on Leadership, The Concise Time Management and Personal Development, The Concise Adair on Teambuilding and Motivation* and *The Concise Adair on Communication and Presentation Skills*.

Contributors

Leadership, teambuilding and innovation

John Adair served in the Arab Legion as adjutant of a Bedouin regiment. After Cambridge University he became Senior Lecturer in Military History and Adviser in Leadership Training at the Royal Military Academy, Sandhurst. In the early 1970s he was Visiting Fellow, Oxford Centre for Management Studies, and in 1979 became Professor in Leadership Studies at the University of Surrey, and later Visiting Professor in Leadership Studies at the University of Exeter. He has worked as a consultant to a wide range of organisations in the UK and overseas, including Shell, Exxon Chemicals, Mercedes-Benz and Unilever. Working over a period of almost a decade with ICI, he helped develop the 'manager-leader' concept, which helped ICI to become the first British company to make a £1 billion profit in 1986. He has conducted seminars in 25 countries.

He is author of numerous leadership and management books (www.john adair. co.uk) including *The Best of Adair on Leadership and Management, The Concise Adair on Leadership, The Concise Time Management and Personal Development, The Concise Adair on Communication and Presentation Skills, The Concise Adair on Teambuilding and Motivation* and *Inspiring Leadership,* all published by Thorogood.

Competitive marketing strategy

Neill Ross MA studied Classics at Cambridge University and after a brief spell in journalism went into publishing, which then became his career. He has spent most of this time in sales and marketing in the UK and overseas in both educational and professional books and journals as well as consumer magazines and publications. He now runs a property business.

Human resources management

Mark Thomas BSc(Econ), Dip PM, MIPM is an international business consultant specialising in strategy, human resource management and managing change. Mark works in Europe, the US and Asia with some of the world's top companies. Before becoming a partner at Performance Dynamics, he worked for several years at Price Waterhouse Management Consultants, where he advised on the business and organisation issues arising from strategic change. His business and consulting experience has included major organisational changes, including mergers and acquisitions, restructuring initiatives and strategic reviews. He is also an accomplished facilitator and speaker who frequently addresses business conferences on a range of issues. He runs Mini-MBA programmes for Falconbury Ltd (www.falconbury.co.uk). Mark has also written several management books: *High Performance Consulting Skills* (Thorogood); *Supercharge Your Management Role – Making the Transition to Internal Consultant* (Butterworth Heinemann); *Mergers and Acquisitions – Confronting the Organisation and People Issues, a special report* (Thorogood); *Project Skills* (Butterworth Heinemann); *Mastering People Management* (Thorogood) and *Gurus on Leadership* (Thorogood).

Finance

Ralph Tiffin is a principal at McLachlan+Tiffin, chartered accountants and registered auditors. The practice has a wide range of clients, and Ralph deals mainly with the larger audit clients. With his background in engineering, Ralph spends approximately one-third of his time lecturing on accounting topics (often related to engineering), project appraisal and management issues in the UK with the Institute of Chemical Engineers, Hawksmere and in-house clients. He also spends up to three months a year lecturing and consulting on similar topics in the Middle East and Asia.

Ralph acts a consultant to many companies in the UK and overseas. Recent projects have included an appraisal of an innovative lightweight tram system. His writing includes *The Complete Guide to International Financial Reporting Standards – 3rd Edition* (Thorogood).

PART ONE

Personal development

1 High achievement

Analysing yourself

The essential ingredients for success are to:

- decide what personal success you want
- create a personal vision of success
- adopt a quantum leap approach
- believe success will happen
- focus on success goals
- be undeterred by setbacks.

The starting point for high achievement in your personal and business life is to review positively your strengths and weaknesses. A basic self-assessment should review:

- What am I good at?
- What do I enjoy doing or would enjoy given the chance?
- What kinds of business would I like to work in or to own?
- What are my assets?
- What work situations, frustrations and stresses do I wish to avoid?

You should ask yourself questions such as these regularly to provide opportunities to focus on what you would like to make happen and to aim for the high achievement of desired results.

Setting goals

High achievement depends on first of all identifying and setting goals, then setting about making them happen by addressing and dealing with those key issues on which success or failure depend.

Three-year goals

- The goal(s) I will achieve within three years are:

  _____

  _____

  _____

  _____

- Subgoal(s) which need to be achieved are:

  _____

  _____

  _____

  _____

One-year goals

- The goal(s) I will achieve within one year are:

  _____

  _____

  _____

  _____

- Subgoal(s) which need to be achieved are:

  _____

  _____

  _____

  _____

In setting these goals you should adopt a quantum leap approach to achieve dramatic results; for example, to triple profits within three years.

You must fix on these goals and use iron determination to make them happen by focusing on the reasons for achieving success:

- My success goals are important to me because:

  _____

  _____

_____

_____

- My success goals are achievable because:

  _____

  _____

  _____

  _____

- The obstacles to be overcome are:

  _____

  _____

  _____

  _____

- The priorities to focus on are:

  _____

  _____

  _____

  _____

2 Time management

Assessing your time-management skills

Time management is not an end in itself. It is the means to an end. When linked with setting and meeting goals it provides a way of getting really high achievement out of individuals and others with whom they come into contact.

How do you rate your time management skills? Do you:

1   Have success goals written down?
    YES/NO

2   Agree your success goals with your boss wherever he or she should be involved?
    YES/NO

3   Give the impression to people that you are well organised, really on top of your job, and still have time for people?
    YES/NO

4   Find enough time to tackle the important projects?
    YES/NO

5   Have a reputation for invariably meeting deadlines?
    YES/NO

6   Ask your PA/Assistant which jobs she or he could do for you?
    YES/NO

7   Work away from the office occasionally to concentrate on a particular job?
    YES/NO

8   Reply to correspondence quickly?
    YES/NO

9   Regularly return telephone calls and emails sufficiently promptly?
    YES/NO

10 Make enough use of technology to save you time?
    YES/NO

11 Deliberately decide to leave certain jobs undone,
   until someone complains?
   YES/NO

12 Make a list of what jobs, telephone calls and emails must or should
   be done today?
   YES/NO

13 Often take work home or go into the office at weekends?
   YES/NO

14 Feel it is better to do a job yourself than to train someone else
   to do it for you?
   YES/NO

15 Allow people to waste your time by dropping in for a chat?
   YES/NO

16 Open the post each morning?
   YES/NO

17 Write things in longhand for you or your PA/Assistant to input?
   YES/NO

18 Spend time doing jobs which a junior person could do as well as you?
   YES/NO

19 Arrange your own meetings?
   YES/NO

20 Waste time filing things or finding files and information?
   YES/NO

21 Sometimes go home feeling the day has been consumed
   by interruptions?
   YES/NO

22 Accept telephone calls during informal meetings?
   YES/NO

23 Spend too much time in unproductive meetings?
   YES/NO

24 Arrive late for meetings quite often?
   YES/NO

25 Spend too much time being chased by others and chasing others
   about missed deadlines?
   YES/NO

26 Think you are too much of a perfectionist for your own good?
   YES/NO

27   Accept requests to do something, when it makes more sense
      for someone else to do it?
      YES/NO

To be rated a 100 per cent effective manager, you should have answered YES to questions 1 to 12 and NO to questions 13 to 27. How did you perform? Is there room for improvement?

Focusing on results and opportunities

In order to use time-management techniques, it is essential to be results-driven and to do this effectively means identifying key results and assessing major opportunities as follows:

Key results to be achieved in order of importance (time spent on them, ranked 1 to 5):

1   deadline:

2   deadline:

3   deadline:

4   deadline:

5   deadline:

The major opportunities to be pursued in order of importance (time spent on them, ranked 1 to 5):

1   deadline:

2   deadline:

3   deadline:

4   deadline:

5   deadline:

Using your diary/organiser for better time management

The trick is to plan your year first and your day last.

1   Enter key year planning dates in your diary/organiser:

   - regular meetings for the year

   - known one-off events (for example, AGM, sales conference, trade fairs, budget preparation)

   - holidays

   - family occasions

   - key tasks (for example, strategic workshop, East Asia visit, customer visits).

2   Plan your next month and:

   - count unplanned days available

   - duck less important events

   - reserve a meeting-free day each week

   - reserve key task time.

3   Plan this week:

   - develop regular habits (for example, weekly team lunch, Friday afternoon in the office).

4   Plan each day at the outset and:

   - develop regular habits

   - fix management-by-walking-about (MBWA) or open door times

   - set personal assistant (PA) times

   - list and rank jobs and phone calls

   - use PA/Assistant to follow up

   - make daily action lists

   - remember 'stress' can be reduced by planning to use your time to tackle areas of concern.

How to manage each day

- Plan each day at the start or better still the night before.

- Make a list of tasks, work out time needed for each and prioritise.

- Isolate the key task and make sure it gets done.

- Don't be too ambitious and clutter each day with tasks that can wait.

- Build a time for solitude and/or to handle an issue that could crop up.

- Reduce interruptions from phone calls, visitors and so on at times earmarked for task completion.

- Tie in each day with the week, the month, the year and your goals.

5   Follow up effectively by using three follow-up files and/or reminders in your diary/organiser:

- this week

- next week

- this month.

6   Diary/daily planning format in print or electronic organiser

Adopt a system which can accommodate detailed timings and sections (in each day) to list 'tasks to be done' and 'phone calls/emails to be made/sent'.

3 Personal effectiveness

This chapter summarises a variety of areas that should be addressed in seeking ways of improving the way you operate in business.

Appearances

You should make your own appearance and that of your office reflect the achievement of your success goals. An action plan is needed for:

- your own appearance – hair, weight, clothes, and so on.
- your office appearance – walls, ceilings, tidiness, decoration.

Create a successful achieving style and remember: you never get a second chance to make a first impression.

Perhaps the most important aspect of appearance (and one which affects the ability to tackle important tasks) is how your desk and computer desktop are managed.

Ways to clear your desk and desktop

- Don't leave any papers on it when you leave.
- Don't have papers out for more than one task at a time.
- Don't keep papers hanging around:
    - diarise when to action and then file them;
    - dump unwanted items;
    - pass on with action notes (handwritten, don't wait for printed formats).
- Don't let filing pile up (do it yourself if need be).
- Don't get side-tracked into reading items that should be put in a separate to-be-read file or pile.
- For computer desktop and emails:
    - use folders for organising material on the desktop

- use folders for 'filing' emails

- keep in-box clear for new items of email

- trash (and empty trash) unwanted items

- filter unwanted items into junk

Handling your manager

It is vital to agree with your own manager (or fellow directors) what will constitute high achievement in your present job.

A key results statement needs to be agreed and results listed in order of importance:

1   **Key result:**

    Standard of performance:

    Priority/deadline:

2   **Key result:**

    Standard of performance:

    Priority/deadline:

3   **Key result:**

    Standard of performance:

    Priority/deadline:

To arrive at this agreed list, you will need to:

- understand the constraints and pressures on your manager

- receive an appraisal of your performance

- negotiate the resources and the support needed to ensure success

- obtain the support needed for high achievement.

You should list the external and internal obstacles to be overcome:

1 Obstacle:

   Action needed:

   Assistance requested from:

2 Obstacle:

   Action needed:

   Assistance requested from:

3 Obstacle:

   Action needed:

   Assistance requested from:

You should agree the major opportunities to pursue and win positive help and commitment to them. A checklist would be:

1 Purpose and results to be achieved:

   _____

   _____

2 Proposal:

   _____

   _____

3 Other tangible benefits to be produced:

   _____

   _____

4 Methods to be adopted:

   _____

   _____

5 Costs and timescale required:

   _____

   _____

6   Financial return to be achieved:

_____

_____

Delegation and teambuilding

It is essential to lead by personal example by:

- defining your goals in writing and believing you will achieve them

- identifying key results

- using your appearance and style to reflect achievement of your success goals

- planning to overcome internal and external obstacles.

You will need to recruit people who will achieve outstanding results and to create and maintain an atmosphere of excitement in which high achievement will flourish. You should ask people whether they:

- want to achieve the key results

- believe they can be achieved

and ask them what will:

- make their jobs more interesting and enjoyable

- have to be done in order to ensure results are achieved

and what can they contribute by way of:

- ideas to overcome difficulties

- ideas for new opportunities to be pursued.

You need to select what to delegate by identifying key tasks and for each one note down:

- which member of your team could do this job

- what exactly is stopping you giving the task away

- what you will do to give the task away effectively.

You should then make lists of:

- tasks to be given away to other team members; and

- extra time which you can then invest in key tasks of your own.

Formats for these lists might be as follows:

Tasks to be given away to other team members:

time to be saved

1 Task:

_____

_____

To be given to:

_____

_____

Action needed:

_____

_____

Target date:

_____

2 Task:

_____

_____

To be given to:

_____

_____

Action needed:

_____

_____

Target date:

_____

3   Task:

_____

_____

To be given to:

_____

_____

Action needed:

_____

_____

Target date:

_____

Extra time to be spent on key tasks:

time to be invested

1   Task:

Action to be taken:

_____

_____

_____

Target date:

_____

2   Task:

Action to be taken:

_____

_____

_____

Target date:

_____

3   Task:

Action to be taken:

_____

_____

_____

Target date:

_____

In order to delegate effectively (once you have identified the time-consuming tasks to delegate and the key tasks to spend more time on), you need to:

- agree the results and the standards to be achieved
- agree the deadlines and the completion dates
- agree any interim check-points
- explain the importance, the context and the constraints
- provide the authority needed
- police the agreed deadlines rigorously
- say thank you when deadlines are met
  - literally
  - write a note
  - with flowers or wine.

You must invest time now to develop your team and should discuss with each person:

- their success goals
- training and development needed
- job satisfaction
- their next job or project.

In respect of training and development programmes, each person should have one and a sensible format is:

Name: Year:

_____

Training to be completed:

_____

_____

Personal development to be completed:

_____

_____

Delegation checklist

- Don't let subordinates 'delegate' to you.
- Don't delegate only the work and not the authority.
- Don't delegate and interfere (other than at agreed checkpoints).
- Don't delegate and forget to follow up.
- Don't delegate without agreeing objectives/results expected.
- Don't delegate and let the problems back rather than the solutions.
- Don't delegate and delay matters by withholding decisions/information.
- Don't delegate without discussing workloads.
- Don't withhold praise.
- Don't do a task if you delegate it.
- Don't confuse delegation with abdication.

Finally, in recruitment, you should remember:

- to replace people incapable of outstanding achievement
- that you have the team you deserve
- to pay well for outstanding achievement
- to recruit resultaholics not workaholics.

To create an atmosphere of excitement to breed high achievement you must:

- exude enthusiasm – it is contagious

- sell not tell key results
- discuss how to make work more enjoyable
  - invite ideas
  - consider prizes/competitions
  - visits to trade shows, branches, and so on
  - sponsored events
- keep people informed of results.

If you aim to reward high achievers (for example, they should be promoted unselfishly because that policy is one of enlightened self-interest), you should also decide to tell people (in private) immediately when their performance falls short, otherwise you are condoning mediocracy.

In summary, the best ways to create a winning team (and create 'free time' for yourself) involve:

- leading by example
- recruiting people for outstanding achievement
- injecting excitement
- giving freedom by delegation
- investing in staff development
- promoting outside your team.

As a brief introduction to the more formal ways of team operation, a structural and results analysis of some different ways of working in teams can be summarised in the following table:

Type of team	Structure and function	Results
Problem-solving team, for example:	• 5-12 volunteers/ employees from different areas of a business or department • meet 1-2 hours per week discuss ways to improve quality, efficiency, etc	• can reduce costs and influence quality • does not result in changes in work efficiency or involve managers enough • fades away over a short period
Special-purpose team, for example:	• design and introduce work reforms and new technology • link all separate functions • involve management, unions, etc. • make operational decisions	• creates high level involvement • can make wide changes
Self-managing team, for example:	• 5-15 employees who produce entire product • members learn all tasks and rotate jobs • members handle all managerial duties	• can increase productivity very significantly (research shows by 30 per cent) • fundamentally changes an organisation • employees more in control of their jobs • eliminates supervisor level

Meetings

Formal meetings

You should first of all test how effective your current formal meetings are by using this checklist:

1   Was the action agreed worth the time spent in preparation, attendance and minute writing?

2   Was the total amount of time spent by those attending justified by the action agreed?

3   Why should the meetings continue to be held?

4   Why do you need to attend the meetings? Why not delegate the job to someone else and attend only when the situation or agenda merits your contribution?

5   Why not hold them quarterly instead of monthly, or monthly instead of weekly, or only when either actual results to date or year-end forecast is more than 5 per cent below budget?

6   Who needs to attend regularly? Who should be invited to attend when relevant? Who only needs to receive the minutes for information?

7   Do you compile or authorise the agenda?

8   Are the agenda and background papers circulated soon enough for people to come adequately prepared?

9   Do the meetings start on time with everyone present?

10 Do you check at the start of the meeting that the actions arising have been completed?

11 How long do the meetings last? How long should they be allowed to last?

12 Do you manage to complete the agenda within the scheduled time regularly?

13 Do people know when the meetings are scheduled to finish? Do they finish on time?

14 Is personal accountability and a deadline assigned to each action item?

15 Why are the minutes not restricted to a list of actions agreed?

16 How soon after the meeting are the minutes circulated? Why aren't they circulated within 24 hours?

17 How long do you spend either writing the minutes or approving them?

18 What percentage of items are actioned by the due date?

19 Why do you tolerate less than 100 per cent?

20 Have you asked those attending the above questions?

You can make your formal meetings more effective by focusing on:

- *Timing*
    - treat starting time as sacrosanct
    - schedule to finish at lunchtime/end of day (any overshoot would be unwelcome to all)
    - only give time to the key issues.

- *Agenda*
    - write it yourself
    - make it specific
    - put important items first
    - circulate in advance (and insist people prepare).

- *Minutes*
    - reduce to action, person responsible and deadline summaries
    - circulate within 24 hours of meeting.

Informal meetings

You should first of all test how effective your current informal meetings are by using this checklist:

1 Do you always telephone to find out when it will be convenient for the other person to meet?

2 When you telephone, do you briefly mention your purpose and agenda so that he/she will be prepared? And indicate how long a discussion is needed? And ask if there is anything else he/she wishes to discuss to ensure you are prepared?

3 Whenever you meet with your manager, if you have a problem, do you always outline the answer you recommend? Are you able to mention the alternatives you have rejected, and your reasons, if asked?

4 Do you hold regular informal meetings with your staff to avoid frequent and unnecessary interruptions?

5 Do you insist that they must never bring a problem to you without having considered the available options and recommending a solution?

6 Do you waste people's time by answering the telephone during informal meetings?

7 Do you ask members of your team to come to your office without the courtesy of telling them your agenda?

8 How often do you visit members of your team rather than have them always visit you?

9 Whenever someone telephones you to suggest a meeting, do you always ask the purpose and the priority needed?

10 Whenever someone visits your office for an informal meeting, do you suggest another time if you are not sufficiently prepared or it will interrupt a key task?

11 Do your meetings always end with decisions approved or specific action and a deadline for completion agreed?

Effective informal meetings usually have this profile:

- telephone in advance to agree
    - purpose
    - agenda
    - convenient time
- attendees should bring problems and answers
- telephone interruptions should be avoided
- decisions should be made with action and deadlines agreed.

Some tips for successfully handling informal meetings include:

- MBWA (management by walking around):
    - you visit your staff (they don't interrupt you)
    - you see for yourself
    - you maintain contact.
- visit people in their offices to meet, rather than letting them visit you, because then you can decide when to leave.
- stand up – sitting can prolong an 'informal' meeting.

The telephone

You must learn to use the telephone to your advantage to ensure that you are using your time effectively and getting results.

Your policy must be only to take calls when and from whom you want. Effective time managers invariably have a policy of not taking incoming calls but operating a call-back system (that is, making the calls when they want and when they are prepared to do so). Key tips are not to receive calls when:

- interviewing
- in an informal meeting
- with a client or a supplier
- in a formal meeting
- you don't want a key task or your creativity to be interrupted.

It is usually better to group calls for a particular time in the day and you should think in advance what you wish each call to achieve. You should reduce time wasted on finding numbers, dialling numbers and making social calls by using your PA to best advantage to call the people you want (and give a list of people, not one at a time) and to keep a good system of regularly updated numbers and best contact times.

You should use your PA to screen callers (and ask 'why?') and to handle routine calls or re-route them. If you are out or don't wish to take a call, your PA should take a message and find out when to call back. Voicemail can be used to the same effect.

Time wasters should be handled by telling them you only have a few minutes (and they should be called at lunchtime or after hours when they are less likely to take up your working time).

Email

- keep in-box for current items only
- use 'folders' to store and track emails
- only deal with important items (some can wait or be delegated)
- handle items at a time to suit you
- don't send them unless absolutely necessary
- indicate clearly where action is required or where they are for information only (and encourage others to do the same to you)
- handle spam so that it does not swamp you by filtering junk mail and trashing it
- do not use if there is a better and quicker way of achieving what you want, eg if a telephone call would be better

- use your PA to handle relevant items including forwarding items to more appropriate people.

Personal productivity

The following is a summary of key ways in which you can boost your own productivity:

In-tray action

- have PA stop unwanted mail
- scrap junk mail
- stop unwanted magazines
- re-route items before they reach you
- remove yourself from unwanted internal circulation lists
- get PA to sort mail into:
  - urgent action
  - team mail
  - reply or action
  - information only
- batch-process correspondence
- scan and dump the unimportant
- separate 'to action' items
- put to one side 'to be read … some time' items
- aim to handle items only once.

Read effectively

- preview long reports by reading the summary, the conclusion/recommendation and scanning the charts/graphs
- read with your eyes – don't subvocalise – and scan and skip
- cope with figures by
  - reading headings
  - looking at the horizontal lines
  - looking at key figures

    –   ignoring uncontentious detail

    –   checking footnotes

    –   asking for exception summary or getting PA to highlight.

Reduce filing (also applies to emails)

- use wastepaper basket
- file address/phone number only
- use central filing for company/team
- put correspondence in date order
- separate bulky reports
- use dividers
- purge and archive
- or dump.

Travel productively

- commute off-peak if possible
- use the time to read and plan your diary
- minimise travel to meetings by having people come to your premises.

Benefit from information technology

Find out as much as you can about and be trained in advance of use of:

- personal computers and the internet
- desk-top publishing
- online information services
- tele and video conferencing
- electronic mailboxes
- internet banking services
- mobile phones and PDAs.

Personal motivation

It is crucial to master ways to motivate yourself, because without self-motivation you will not only fail to achieve your goals but you will also fail to motivate others to help you to achieve them. What follows is a self-motivation checklist (to be used whenever you feel your motivation is flagging).

Self-motivation checklist

- Focus on your goals and keep difficulties in perspective.
- See your problems as opportunities.
- Become a resultaholic not a workaholic.
- Set deadlines.
- Work on the important not the seemingly urgent.
- Take time out to think.
- Develop non-work interests and activities.
- Write down your fears/problems/frustrations and ways of overcoming them.
- Don't pass over a difficult task – start the day with it, or fix a time to do it.

The whole area of self-motivation requires separate study, but if you are experiencing a real motivation crisis, you should refer back to chapter 1 on high achievement to try to focus on what you want to achieve.

Remember, too, that current research shows that the left side of your brain can be in 'conflict' with the right. You should be aiming to address certain self-motivation difficulties by using each part of the brain to compensate for the difficulties caused by the other.

Here is a comparison of the characteristics of the left and right sides of the brain:

'LEFT' BRAIN (dominant side)

- controls right side of body
- verbal
- rational, controlled
- logical
- reading, writing

- naming
- mathematical/scientific

'RIGHT' BRAIN

- controls left side of body
- non-verbal
- non-rational, emotional
- intuitive, creative
- face recognition
- artistic, musical, songs, understands humour

A useful technique to 'change your way of thinking' about a situation, particularly when you feel demotivated, is to change a negative thought pattern into a positive one.

Negative approach

- I can't
- I should
- I hope
- It's not my fault
- It's a problem
- It's difficult
- If only
- It's terrible
- What can I do?

Positive approach

- I won't
- I could
- I know
- I am responsible
- It's an opportunity
- It's a challenge

- Next time, I will
- It's a learning experience
- I know I can cope

Business knowledge

High achieving managers need to ensure that they develop an effective knowledge of their business and the environment it operates in. To have an improving approach you should:

- read the trade press regularly, on-line when possible

- use the internet to look at competitor, supplier and customer websites to increase your knowledge of them

- scan the technical pages of relevant newspapers/websites to look for developments which may affect your business

- maintain links with relevant university research departments or industry research associations

- make sure you have the opportunity to meet major customers even if you are no longer directly involved in sales

- visit the point of sale for your products occasionally – for example, the wholesaler, retail outlet, website, or your own branch – to know what is happening

- meet with existing and potential suppliers occasionally to find out about their developments

- visit the major exhibitions in your industry sector to keep informed about competitors

- visit other countries to meet overseas competitors, or to find new sources of supply, or to assess export opportunities, or to find out what is happening there at first hand

- listen to your sales people to keep informed about your competitors

- ask your customers about the opportunities and pressures facing them so that you can respond to their needs.

The effective manager

As a reminder to yourself, you should keep in mind these ten qualities which research has shown are the hallmarks of the effective manager:

1   Provide clear direction.

2   Use two-way communication.

3   Demonstrate high integrity.

4   Choose the right people.

5   Coach and support people.

6   Give objective recognition.

7   Establish controls.

8   Understand the financial implications of decisions.

9   Encourage new ideas and innovation.

10   Give clear decisions when needed.

4 Leadership

There is (has been and probably always will be) a debate about the differences and overlaps of leadership and management. Current opinion is that they are different concepts but they overlap considerably.

Leadership has five distinctive characteristics not found in management. A leader must:

1 give direction
2 provide inspiration
3 build teams
4 set an example
5 be accepted.

Henri Fayol (in 1916) listed the qualities needed by a person in 'command'. Such a person should:

- have a thorough knowledge of employees
- eliminate the incompetent
- be well versed in the agreements binding the business and its employees
- set a good example
- conduct periodic audits of the organisation and use summarised charts to further this review
- bring together the chief assistants by means of conferences at which unity of direction and focusing of effort are provided for
- not become engrossed in detail
- aim at making unity, energy, initiative and loyalty prevail among all employees.

Seven qualities of leadership

1 Enthusiasm: try naming a leader without it!
2 Integrity: meaning both personal wholeness and sticking to values outside yourself, primarily goodness and truth – this quality makes people trust a leader.

3   Toughness: demanding, with high standards, resilient, tenacious and with the aim of being respected (not necessarily popular).

4   Fairness: impartial, rewarding or penalising performance without 'favourites', treating individuals differently but equally.

5   Warmth: having the heart as well as the mind engaged, loving what is being done and caring for people – cold fish do not make good leaders.

6   Humility: the opposite of arrogance, being a listener and without an overwhelming ego.

7   Confidence: not over-confidence (which leads to arrogance) but self-confidence – people know whether you have or have not got it.

Functions of leadership

In leadership, there are always three elements or variables:

1   The leader: qualities of personality and character.

2   The situation: partly constant, partly varying.

3   The group: the followers, their needs and values.

This chapter looks at leadership functions in relation to the needs of work groups. There are three overlapping needs.

1   Task needs: to achieve the common task.

2   Team maintenance needs: to hold together or maintain the team.

3   Individual needs: those which individuals bring with them into the group.

These three needs (task, team and individual) are the watchwords of leadership. People expect their leaders to:

*   help them achieve the common task

*   build the synergy of teamwork, and

*   respond to individuals and meet their needs.

The task needs include the setting up of work groups or organisations because the task cannot be done by one person alone. The task has needs because pressure is built up to accomplish it to avoid frustration in the people involved if they are prevented from completing it.

The team maintenance needs are the creation, promotion and retention of group/organisational cohesiveness, which are essential on the 'united we stand, divided we fall' principle.

The individual needs are physical (salary and bonus) and psychological:

- recognition
- a sense of doing something worthwhile
- status
- the deeper need to give and to receive from other people in a working situation.

The task, team and individual needs overlap (see Figure 4.1).

This overlapping is evident in that:

- achieving the task builds the team and satisfies the individuals
- if team maintenance fails (the team lacks cohesiveness), performance of the task is impaired and individual satisfaction is reduced
- if individual needs are not met, the team will lack cohesiveness and performance of the task will be impaired.

Leadership exists at different levels:

- **Team leadership:** of teams of 5-20 people

Figure 4.1   John Adair's Three Circles of Functional (Action-centred) Leadership

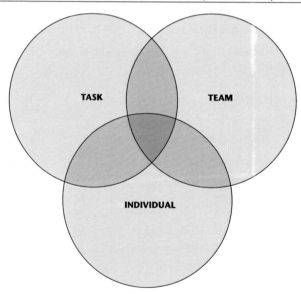

- **Operational leadership:** essential in a business or organisation comprising a number of teams whose leaders report to you
- **Strategic leadership:** a whole business or organisation, with overall accountability for the levels of leadership below you.

Whatever the level of leadership, task, team and individual needs must be constantly thought about. To achieve the common task, maintain teamwork and satisfy the individuals, certain functions have to be performed. A function is what leaders do as opposed to a quality which is an aspect of what they are.

These functions (the functional approach to leadership, also called action-centred leadership) are:

- defining the task
- planning
- briefing
- controlling
- evaluating
- motivating
- organising
- providing an example.

5 Teambuilding

This chapter looks at teambuilding – part of the task, team and individual trinity – from the leadership perspective.

One of the main results of good leadership is a good team.

As far back as 1985, ICI believed that the outcomes of effective leadership were that people would:

- have a clear sense of direction and work hard and effectively
- have confidence in their ability to achieve specific challenging objectives
- believe in and be identified with the organisation
- hold together when the going is rough
- have respect for and trust in managers
- adapt to the changing world.

In achieving the task, building the team and developing the individual, although leadership style may differ, effective leaders (as emphasised in ICI's findings and its development courses) must:

- feel personally responsible for his/her human, financial and material resources
- be active in setting direction and accepting the risks of leadership
- be able to articulate direction and objectives clearly and keep his/her people in the picture
- use the appropriate behaviour and methods to gain commitment for the achievement of specific objectives
- maintain high standards of personal performance and demand high standards of performance from others.

Leaders in teambuilding provide the functions of:

- planning
- initiating
- controlling
- supporting

- informing
- evaluating.

The good leader in teambuilding must act as:

- encourager
- harmoniser
- compromiser
- expediter/gatekeeper
- standard setter
- group observer/commentator
- follower.

6 Mentoring and coaching

Mentoring and coaching should be vitally important parts of your career development. They are widely used by chief executives of listed companies, entrepreneurs, financial directors, partners in professional firms and executives of public-sector and not-for-profit organisations. You may be none of these yet, but you can still derive substantial benefits, even if you have not got your first managerial job.

A mentor and a coach can help you as a:

- sounding board
  - to address and evaluate major opportunities and problems rigorously and dispassionately
- counsellor and confidante
  - to deal with emotional and relationship issues at work
- constructive challenger
  - to give you candid feedback
- coach and trainer
  - to improve your approach and to identify your training needs
- powerful inspiration
  - to inspire you to improve your achievement dramatically and to support you when the going gets tough
- career adviser
  - to set career goals and achieve them either within the company or elsewhere
- networker
  - to help develop your networking skills and introduce you to useful contacts
- life coach
  - to achieve a more satisfying work-life balance.

Chief executives and senior executives readily pay for costly coaching and mentoring because it delivers tangible benefits for their company and themselves. For other staff, however, there is no need to pay a mentor and coach for them to enjoy similar benefits.

Potential mentors and coaches available to you include:

- a previous manager in another company
  - this could work extremely well because he/she knows you well and has no conflict of interest

- a family friend
  - ideally, the person should be a successful executive who knows you well and has your respect

- a networking contact
  - you may have met a senior executive in your industry sector, or someone in a different field, and feel there is sufficient rapport to request the help you want

- your previous manager within the company
  - he or she should be dispassionate, but some conflict could arise. You should seek the agreement of your immediate manager at the outset, and there is a possible risk that your mentor may give feedback to your manager which you would not want

- your immediate manager
  - every manager should act as a coach and mentor to staff reporting directly to him or her. The disadvantage is that the manager cannot be expected to act solely in your best interest, because this could conflict with departmental or company needs

- a parent
  - some people use a parent with senior executive experience as a mentor and coach. Arguably, however, the relationship is too close. If you doubt this, just remember the difficulty people so often have when a parent teaches them to drive a car.

For mentoring and coaching to be really effective, informal ground rules need to agreed at the outset, including:

- you, not your mentor, should set the agenda for discussion, but this should not preclude your mentor from occasionally raising issues which need to be aired

- your mentor should help you to come to your own solutions, and not give you ready-made answers

- your mentor should recognise that you may have different ambitions, priorities and commitment from him/her

- your mentor should challenge you and to be candid with you, but in a supportive way.

For you to benefit from a mentor and coach, you need to answer the following questions:

- What specific benefits do I want to achieve?

  _____

  _____

- Who could be my mentor?

  _____

  _____

- What will I do to make it happen?

  _____

  _____

You can benefit substantially not only by having your own mentor and coach but also by becoming a mentor and coach yourself.

If you are already a manager, every person reporting directly to you has a right to expect you to adopt a coaching and mentoring style of management. Command and control is the essence of management in the armed forces, but it has no role in the modern workplace.

If you are not yet a manager, volunteer to be a mentor and coach to a new graduate, not necessarily in your department, or someone joining your department in a less senior role than yours. The benefits to you include:

- you will learn an invaluable management skill
- your initiative will help single you out as someone with demonstrable management potential
- you are likely to find it satisfying and enjoyable.

To make a start as a mentor and coach within your organisation, you need to answer the following questions:

- What will I do to learn more about mentoring and coaching from the internet or magazine articles?

  _____

  _____

- Who is an effective mentor and coach in my organisation I can learn from?

  _____

  _____

- What do I need to do to commence mentoring and coaching?

  _____

  _____

7 Solving problems and decision-making

Effective decision-making

To be an effective decision-maker:

- you should identify the decisions which if made:
    - will have the biggest impact on the key results
    - will achieve a quantum leap improvement in excess of the key results which have been set.

- when making a decision, you should ask:
    - what result will be achieved?
    - what is the fundamental purpose?
    - what other options/opportunities should be exposed?

- you should consider the issues and identify:
    - what could go wrong
    - the obstacles you may face
    - any likely hostile response by competitors, trades unions, staff, etc.

- you should challenge the status quo:
    - why do it?
    - why not do it?
    - why this often?
    - why this standard?
    - why this way?
    - why here?
    - why this price/cost?

- you should always make decisions in time for them to be effective.

Solving problems

- The difficulties faced in solving problems can include:
  - too much information
  - spending time fact-finding
  - not identifying key data required
  - not planning ahead
  - last-minute realisation of time difficulties
  - not having adequate data
  - not recognizing useful ideas
  - doubting your own
  - ignoring others.
- Successful approaches to problem solving lie in part in correcting the above problems by
  - clearly identifying the problem
  - writing it down
  - establishing the facts and objectives
  - considering a wide range of solutions
  - calmly reviewing options and ideas
  - focusing on results and desired outcome and not preventing solutions from presenting themselves
  - objectively choosing the best solution.
- Brainstorming:
  - individual brainstorming
  - write down the problem
  - write down at least 20 ideas and their opposites
  - use lateral thinking (seemingly unrelated ideas)
  - prioritise choose the best ideas
  - group brainstorming
  - appoint 'recorder'
  - identify problem clearly in writing
  - allow free-flow (no criticism as you go) of ideas
  - select ideas to pursue
  - arrange follow-up action meeting.

Handling crises

You should have your own personal approach to crisis management, to deal with crises as they will arise in business.

A helpful checklist is provided below for you to refer to at such times, but you should first of all check whether you are good or bad at avoiding crises.

How to avoid a crisis:

- have a plan to handle potential crises (for example, computer failure, post strikes, employee strikes, fire)
- anticipate change (do not merely respond when it happens)
- do not delay making decisions hoping a problem will go away
- do not respond to minor difficulties as if they were major crises
- remember that if a crisis happens you should respond calmly but urgently.

How to handle a crisis:

- individually or collectively agree its identity and seriousness – define the problem
- state desired result
- list solutions
- test the feasibility of preferred solutions
- choose and implement an action plan without delay.

8 Innovation

It is worth identifying some of the key players who, if they were all present within it, would surely make an organisation unbeatable:

- Creative thinker: produces new and original ideas
- Innovator: brings new products or services to the market or changes existing ones
- Inventor: produces new and commercial ideas
- Entrepreneur: conceives or receives ideas and translates them into business reality to exploit a market opportunity
- Intrapreneur: responsible for innovation within an organisation
- Champion: has determination and commitment to implement an idea
- Sponsor: backs an idea and helps remove obstacles.

Successful businesses run on innovation and change and effective innovation requires:

- a blend of new ideas
- the ability to get things done
- sound commercial sense
- customer focus
- a conducive organisational climate.

Managers should be able to:

- manage for creativity
- provide an organisational environment in which innovation can thrive
- use a variety of techniques to stimulate ideas for products, services or systems and to generate ideas for bringing them to fruition.

Managing innovation

To manage innovation (and draw 'greatness' out of people), it must be seen as a process with three phases:

1   The generation of ideas (from individuals and teams)

2   The harvesting of ideas (people evaluating ideas)

3   The implementation of ideas (teams developing and introducing ideas to the final, customer-satisfied stage).

Remember that creative thinking makes innovation possible and teamwork makes it happen. Successful innovation requires an organisation and its key managers to be able to perform five essential functions:

Recruiting and selecting creative people

For the appropriate jobs, of course, you will need creative people. Their characteristics tend to be:

* high general intelligence

* strong motivation

* stimulated by challenge

* vocational attitude to work

* able to hold contradictory ideas together in creative tension

* curious with good listening and observing skills

* able to think for themselves (independent thinkers)

* neither introvert nor extrovert, but rather in the middle

* interested in many things.

Encouraging creativity in teams

It is not always easy to manage the creative and innovative aspects of teamwork. Ideally, individuals need to share the values, characteristics and interests of the other team members in order to work with them in harmony and yet have something different to offer.

Encouraging creativity in teams (besides helping individuals to 'perform' the Belbin roles within a team) depends on a manager's skills in:

* using the different skills within the team (having first identified the attributes of each individual)

- ensuring conflicts of ideas are allowed to happen and are tolerated by all

- recognising particularly good contributions

- helping the team generate ideas (for example, by brainstorming)

- creating an open environment where individuals can speak honestly.

Team training

Self-evidently important (to improve team performance) is the development of team creativity by improving an individual's skills in effective thinking and communication in his/her own particular area of expertise/specialism.

Communicating about innovation

Feedback can maintain interest levels and information about progress made can stimulate further activity and more progress. Good communication can help improve creativity and innovation and should:

- stress the importance of new ideas and show how business has improved because of their implementation

- indicate why ideas have been rejected/accepted

- give progress reports of ideas originated by individuals/teams

- recognise and reward appropriately for successful innovation.

Overcoming obstacles to innovation

Managers must ensure that creativity and innovation are not killed off by:

- an initial response of outright condemnation, ridicule, rejection, damning criticism or faint praise

- the vested interest of a particular person or department

- too early an evaluation or judgement – sometimes suspending judgement early on allows an idea to grow and reach a stage where it will work.

Managers who are creative and act in innovation-friendly ways not only have the usual leadership skills (of defining objectives, planning, controlling, supporting and reviewing in the areas of task, team and individual needs) but also are able to:

- accept risk

- work with half-formed ideas

- bend the rules

- respond quickly
- be enthusiastic (to motivate others).

Organisations and innovation

The business organisation itself has to provide an environment in which creativity and innovation can flourish. The five characteristics of organisations that are good at innovation (and do not just pay lip service to it) are:

1 top-level commitment

2 a flexible organisational structure

3 tolerance of failure (not risk averse)

4 encouragement of teamwork and innovation

5 open and constructive communication.

Characteristics of innovators

As a manager you should possess the following skills and qualities:

- a clear vision of required results
- the ability to:
  - define objectives and benefits of ideas/projects
  - present the case for it powerfully
  - win support from superiors, colleagues and subordinates
  - motivate people into action so that they contribute to project success
  - influence others to support the project
  - deal with criticism, interference, lack of enthusiasm, disputes and lateness
- courage – to take risks (and endure any setbacks)
- willpower – to maintain momentum
- fairness – to ensure all who participate are recognised and rewarded.

9 Effective communication skills

Effective writing (letters/emails/reports/plans)

- Avoid writing whenever possible
  - don't merely confirm or acknowledge
  - telephone rather than write/email
  - produce standard paragraphs for your PA to use
  - your PA should write routine letters/emails
  - don't always write/email to team members, speak to them.
- Write clearly
  - use headings
  - use short sentences
  - itemise individual points
  - use short paragraphs
  - don't be frightened of writing one-sentence letters/emails
  - be informal.
- Effective reports
  - start with an executive summary
  - summarise recommendation
  - outline financial justification and benefit
  - use precise key points and figures only
  - must make sense on their own
  - bind them
  - have a contents page
  - number the pages
  - use dividers
  - relegate the back-up information to appendices
  - avoid 90 degree turns.

- Business plans
    - see Chapters 14 and 15 on strategy and on business plans.

Effective presentations

There are four essential steps to take to ensure that presentations in different situations are successful. They are: preparation, gaining and keeping attention, maintaining interest and closing positively.

Effective preparation

- Informal presentation/meetings
    - define the desired outcome (check out support of key team members, if appropriate)
    - set the agenda (circulate if appropriate)
    - gather the data
    - spell out the benefits
    - summarise financial justification.
- Formal presentations
    - check out the venue and set up (numbers attending, lay-out, equipment available, and so on)
    - check time available for your presentation and how you will be introduced
    - check out who will attend and get background on them
    - rehearse your presentation (and check on visuals, and so on)
    - expect to be nervous (but remember that 'nerves' will fade after a few minutes)
    - try to meet attendees before your 'session' so that you will 'know' them.

Gaining and keeping attention

- Informal presentations/meetings
    - fix the best (most convenient/distraction free) place
    - only start when you have the complete attention of the others
    - agree start and finish times
    - ensure there are no interruptions.

- Formal presentations
    - make sure the audience is ready and seated before you start
    - deliver your opening sentence positively to command attention.

Maintaining interest

- Informal presentations/meetings
    - don't waffle; stick to the point
    - involve other people
    - focus on 'good news' and benefits
    - mention key opportunities/results/issues in a way that will command attention
    - convince by showing financial justification, how it will work in practice and what the evidence is that it will work
    - talk with conviction.
- Formal presentations
    - tell people why the subject is important to them
    - tell them the topics you will cover (and when you would like to take questions – throughout or at the end)
    - advise them of the decision/approval you expect, if appropriate
    - use flip-charts/slides/computer presentations/videos to hold audience concentration
    - use key words on visuals
    - don't read your presentation
    - demonstrate your own conviction and enthusiasm in words, voice and gesture
    - spell out benefits
    - present factual evidence (not opinions)
    - demonstrate financial justification
    - show that potential problems have been identified and overcome
    - handle questions as arranged and authoritatively.

Closing positively

- Informal presentations/meetings
    - close with agreement to the outcome you want

- agree who will do what by when
- if there is no agreement, try to ensure that some positive action is taken towards your goal.

- Formal presentations
  - ask for the approval, order or action you want to conclude your presentation.

General advice on presentations

- Rehearse, rehearse, rehearse.
- Use computer visuals or slides or flip-charts if possible
  - help structure presentation
  - allow audience to focus on key points
  - let you look at audience while elaborating on the key points
  - keep information on each visual to a minimum (20 words or fewer figures)
  - make sure type on visuals is big enough to be seen clearly
  - show visuals in correct order (and number them)
  - use visual stimulus, such as cartoons.
- Work on your presentational style
  - entertain your audience with anecdotes, illustrations, examples
  - vary your voice (tone and level)
  - use 'jokes' sparingly if at all
  - avoid bad language, risqué jokes, and so on.
  - avoid excessive walking about or extravagant gestures
  - involve your audience; let them question you, but also question them; don't hold on to fixed ideas, listen
  - let them hear, see and do: lecture, visual aids, worked examples/ syndicate discussions, and so on.
  - don't apologise
  - relax.

10 Personal marketing and public relations

Virtually every business, from multinational companies to self-employed sole traders, markets its products and services. Automobile manufacturers spend billions every year on marketing because it sells more vehicles and increases profits. Yet only a small proportion of people deliberately market and promote themselves, and those who do it effectively really do accelerate their career and earning power.

Personal marketing and public relations (PR) needs to target separately:

- your own company
- the wider market.

Within your own company

Become more widely known and respected by:

- becoming an expert or a guru
- volunteering for high-profile project teams or working parties
- being recognised as someone who sees and pursues the big picture by thinking, talking and acting strategically.

Become an expert or a guru

Your aim should be to become an expert within your own department, so that colleagues and even your manager consult you. For example, when a new piece of software is installed, such as a new diary management system, make a point of becoming 'the expert' and offer help to other colleagues. Better still, become an expert in something where people outside of your department, especially senior managers, are keen to get your help. You may be a finance manager and take the opportunity to become 'the guru' on new software for budgeting.

Volunteer for project teams and working parties

Ideally, seek project teams and working parties which cross departmental boundaries and involve senior managers. The object is to be noticed without being seen as pushy. As with becoming an expert or a guru, there will be opportunities for networking with people from other departments, particularly high achievers and senior managers.

Be a big-picture person

Always portray yourself as someone who looks at problems, issues and opportunities within the wider context of the company or group, rather than taking a personal stance, which could be interpreted as selfish, or merely a departmental view, which may be seen as blinkered.

You need to think, talk and act strategically at all times. Before speaking up make sure you have considered the wider implications and the knock-on effects elsewhere in the company. For example, before you request approval to reward your team with a dinner to recognise their hard work and success, consider whether this is likely to set a precedent which other people will copy and take advantage of even though it is not really justified.

Formulate your action plan as follows:

- What am I an expert or a guru on already?

  _____

  _____

- What will I do to become more widely recognised and respected for it?

  _____

  _____

- What opportunities exist for me to become an expert or a guru?

  _____

  _____

- What will I do to become widely recognised and respected for it?

  _____

  _____

* How can I become aware of high-profile project team and working party opportunities?

  _____

  _____

* What opportunities will arise to demonstrate I am a big-picture person?

  _____

  _____

* How can I network more effectively within the company or group?

  _____

  _____

In the wider market

There are various opportunities for effective personal marketing and PR, such as:

* writing articles or blogs
* public speaking
* trade association or professional body activities
* social networking sites
* becoming known to headhunters
* charity work
* alumni events.

Writing articles and blogs

Trade magazines and the journals of professional bodies in print and on-line formats welcome contributions, but serendipity won't work for you. Don't wait for an invitation, contact the relevant website, magazine or journal.

Find out their readership profile by requesting an advertising pack. This will segment the readership into categories, such as directors, business owners, senior managers, and by size of company. It will contain a couple of back issues or other background information, so analyse the type of article/blog most likely to be published and identify which person to telephone or email, such as the editor, features editor or commissioning editor. Ask what topics are currently relevant for their readers, and be ready to offer appropriate ideas or to phone back if you need time to develop other ideas. All this will be more readily apparent by looking on-line.

Customer or client success stories are popular and provide the opportunity to showcase your products or services. Make sure, however, that your article/blog features your customer or client in a favourable light, not you, and obtain complimentary attributable quotes. You will always need to get the prior approval of your immediate manager, who in turn may have to obtain approval from the corporate communications department. Even more important, you will need to get the go-ahead from your client before writing an article or blog, and obtain written approval before submitting it to a magazine.

For personal PR impact, you need to get the magazine (or website) to confirm that a footnote (or click through) will give your contact details – your email address at least and preferably a direct line telephone number as well.

Develop your own blogging activities for your company and by posting comments on other blogs/sites. Also participate where appropriate in other relevant company/individual social networking activities, e.g. through Twitter, Facebook or Linkedin.

Personal procrastination is your real enemy, so develop your ideas and action plan by answering the following questions:

- Which magazines or journals (including websites) should I target?

  _____

  _____

- Whom do I need to contact in each one?

  _____

  _____

- What ideas or topics will I offer them?

  _____

  _____

Public speaking

Remember the show-business adage 'Overnight success at the London Palladium or Caesar's Palace, Las Vegas often requires years of appearing in pubs and clubs'. Don't expect to start by being invited to present at a major international conference. Seize every opportunity to speak to an audience. Gain your confidence by:

- volunteering to give a vote of thanks

- presenting at a departmental meeting

- contributing to in-house training courses

- talking to a branch meeting of your trade association or professional body

As soon as you feel ready, however, identify relevant conference organisers, find out who devises the programme content and invites the speakers, then offer to speak. Conference organisers often struggle to find speakers, especially people able to present a real-life case study, and you may well be pleasantly surprised by their receptiveness. As with writing for publication, you will need company approval, but it probably makes sense to get an invitation first.

The questions you need to answer are:

- Which professional bodies or conference organisers present you with relevant public speaking opportunities?

  _____

  _____

- Who is the person responsible for finding suitable speakers?

  _____

  _____

- What topics or case studies will you offer to present?

  _____

  _____

Trade association or professional body activities

Volunteer to attend social functions because they offer powerful networking opportunities and your colleagues may dismiss them as a waste of time. Attend branch meetings or special interest groups, and be ready to join the organising committee. Who knows, you may end up as regional chairperson or even European president of your trade association. Apathy is rife, so positive action will pay dividends for you.

The questions to be answered include:

- Which professional bodies, trade associations or business clubs are relevant for you?

  _____

  _____

- What social events should you attend?

  _____

  _____

- What do you need to do to become an official?

  _____

  _____

Social networking sites

In this context social networking sites such as Linkedin and its 'groups' can be helpful as a way of furthering contacts in chosen trade or professional areas. It can also help with activity in the next section.

Becoming known to headhunters

You need to be known to the relevant headhunters. Arguably, the best time to contact them is when you are not seeking a career move! You should identify the relevant person to contact and telephone or email to suggest meeting for a coffee so that you can outline your career goals and obtain their advice, making it clear that you are not looking for another job right now. The flattery of asking for career advice will work and you are likely to get valuable guidance as well. Subsequently, keep in touch by informing them of your promotion or job changes.

The questions to be answered include:

- Which head-hunting firms are most relevant for your next career move?

  _____

  _____

- Which person is the most appropriate to contact in each firm?

  _____

  _____

Charity work

Charity work is rewarding and socially enjoyable, but it can also be powerful personal PR. Use the internet to identify charity organisations and projects which involve captains of industry, or at least, senior directors. They always need people to help organise events, so be ready to volunteer. Age or lack of seniority are no bar to your involvement, but select a cause that you care about.

Turn good intention into positive achievement by answering the following questions:

- Which charitable organisations and events interest me and are high profile?

  _____

  _____

  _____

- Who should I telephone to offer my help?

  _____

  _____

  _____

Alumni events

You should consider attending social events organised by your alumni groups (schools, universities and business schools), professional bodies and former employers, such as accounting firms or management consultants. Equally, you should not rule out volunteering for an organising role.

To sum up

You may find the recommended action is too calculating and too pushy. Nonsense! These initiatives are powerful, will accelerate your career and will be seen as totally professional when done with a touch of finesse.

PART TWO

Management skills

11 Finance

This chapter concentrates on the practical finance and accounting techniques needed to manage for profit and to generate the maximum cash flow from a business. It is divided into two main parts which describe the elements required for sound commercial practice:

1 Technical aspects which need to be understood.

2 Techniques which can be applied.

Understanding the essentials

The profit and loss account

There are usually presentational differences between 'internal' profit and loss accounts (prepared for management use within a company, usually monthly) and 'external' profit and loss accounts, which form part of a company's annual financial statements.

Basically, the profit and loss account is a statement of the income receivable during a given period and the costs incurred in generating that income. The difference is the profit or loss. (It is the income receivable and not necessarily received in cash during the period. Similarly, it is costs incurred but not necessarily paid during the period.)

An 'internal' profit and loss account will generally focus on:

Turnover (sales or revenue) A

less

Direct costs		B
Gross profit	=	C

less

Depreciation		
Provisions		D
Overheads		
Net profit	=	E

For management purposes, the detail and the format will vary from business to business. What matters is that a profit and loss account should give an accurate picture. This will enable the various component elements to be tracked so that appropriate decisions and action can be taken.

The external (published or statutory) profit and loss account has none of the detail of management accounts but has by law to disclose certain elements of income and expense:

- turnover (a UK term for sales or revenue)
- some information on costs
- bank interest, payable and receivable
- taxation payable
- dividends to shareholders
- profit retained in the business to finance growth.

In essence, the profit or loss is calculated by:

- the sales turnover or fee income invoiced (but not necessarily received from customers during the year)

less the total of

- the costs incurred to produce the invoiced sales turnover or fee income (but not necessarily paid during the year)

and

- the depreciation charged on assets owned by the business during the year.

Depreciation is a charge made to the profit and loss account with a similar reduction in the asset value or amount reflected in the balance sheet. Depreciation is a charge for the 'consumption' of the asset; that is, a portion of the cost of the asset used is matched with the income generated by the use of the asset. Depreciation is frequently calculated on a 'straight-line basis'. The cost (less any estimated realisable value on disposal) is divided by the estimated number of years of useful life of the asset. See later for more details.

It is almost certain that the profit made by a business and the amount of cash generated will be different. Although the profit and loss account is based on cash received and paid out during the financial year it also includes:

- income invoiced and not received

- costs incurred and not paid (these have to be accrued)
- the cost of depreciation (not a cash movement)
- changes in levels of stock

Indeed, a profitable manufacturing company may consume cash during a period of expansion, because additional finance may be needed for:

- increased stocks of raw materials and finished goods
- the increased level of work-in-progress in the factory
- a larger amount of money owed by customers, which is described as debtors
- investment in capital equipment.

It would be reasonable to assume that there is a standardised format for all profit and loss accounts, but it would be wrong. The presentation is broadly similar, but it is important not to be confused by different presentations.

A simple form of published profit and loss account is as shown below:

For the years ending 31 December	Latest year	Previous year
	£m	£m
Turnover	603	570
Operating costs	540	515
Operating profit	63	55
Net interest payable	(9)	(12)
Profit on ordinary activities before taxation	54	43
Taxation on profit on ordinary activities	14	12
Profit attributable to ordinary shareholders	40	31
Dividends	13	10
Retained profit transferred to reserves	27	21

The published profit and loss account and the balance sheet need to be read in conjunction with the accounting policies and the notes to the accounts that accompany them in the Annual Report (see below) of each company.

The **Annual Report** contains the:

- CEO's or chairman's statement
- report of the directors
- statement of accounting policies
- audited profit and loss account, balance sheet, and cash flow statement
- notes to the accounts, providing supplementary information
- in the case of stockmarket-listed companies, often historical performance figures over the past five or ten years.

The accounting policies explain the basis on which the accounts have been prepared, for example the method used to value stocks and work in progress.

The notes to the accounts provide the detail behind some of the figures shown in the profit and loss account and balance sheet, together with other supplementary information, such as details of directors' remuneration.

Typical descriptions of the terms used in the profit and loss account shown above are:

1 *Turnover*: sales invoiced to customers during the financial year, excluding value-added tax (VAT). Only sales to third parties are taken into account for the profit and loss account of a group.

2 *Operating costs*: consist of several items such as:

- cost of goods and services invoiced
- distribution costs
- research and development
- administrative and other expenses
- employees' profit-sharing bonus.

3 *Operating profit*: the profit on the normal trading activities of the company, before taking into account bank interest and taxation.

4 *Net interest payable*: the net amount of interest receivable and payable on all overdrafts, loans, etc.

5 *Profit on ordinary activities before taxation*: the profit before tax

6 *Taxation on profit on ordinary activities*: based on the profit for the year and takes into account deferred taxation which arises from timing differences between the taxation rules and accounting policies used

by the company. These timing differences are common, for example, between capital allowances for taxation and depreciation.

7   *Profit attributable to ordinary shareholders*: profit earned for the ordinary shareholders, after charging the liability for taxation arising on the profits.

8   *Dividends*: the total cost of the dividend paid to ordinary shareholders.

9   *Retained profit transferred to reserves*: profit after tax left in the business to provide additional finance for future growth and development.

Published profit and loss accounts often seem more complicated in real life. The problem is the enormous amount of disclosure required by law under national and international accounting standards. Although the figures may be daunting, a patient analysis should reveal what is happening – do ignore immaterial figures!

Some other terms include:

10 *Other operating income*: examples might be government grants, royalties and other income.

11 *Share of profits less losses of related companies (associated companies or joint ventures)*: these are companies in which the owning company owns between 20 and 50 per cent of the shares, and exercises significant influence on commercial and financial policy decisions. The share of profits consists of:

   •   dividend income

   •   share of undistributed profits less losses

   •   gains on disposal of investments

   •   amounts written off investments.

12 *Attributable to minorities*: the share of profits on ordinary activities after taxation to which minority shareholders in subsidiary companies are entitled.

A subsidiary company is a company between 50 and 100 per cent of which is owned by a holding company, which means effective management control is exercised.

13 *Extraordinary items*: events or transactions outside the ordinary activities of the business which are both material and not expected to reoccur frequently or regularly. However, as many companies have tried to pass off bad news as 'extraordinary' the accounting standard setters have effectively banned the use of this heading.

14 *One-off profits or losses, reorganisation costs, profit on sale of property, and so on*: should be shown separately below the line of trading profit. These items are considered to occur in the normal course of business (they are NOT extraordinary) – their size makes them significant and they are classified as exceptional items.

15 *Preference dividend*: the dividend payable on preference shares, which are usually entitled to receive the same amount of dividend each year.

Depreciation

Depreciation is charged on tangible fixed assets, such as machinery, equipment, vehicles and buildings, but not on land. For intangible assets (see below) the term amortisation is used. Depreciation is included as part of the operating costs. The most commonly used method to calculate it is to write off the cost of the asset evenly over its estimated useful life, where appropriate taking into account any residual value likely to be realised on disposal.

Intangible assets are items capitalised on the balance sheet – that is, items which are treated as assets not costs when purchased. Examples of intangible assets are goodwill, brand names, research and development, and intellectual property, such as patents. Only purchased intangibles should be capitalised. Internally generated goodwill, patents and so on have to be written off as costs. Capitalised intangibles should be amortised over a period not normally exceeding 20 years.

Depreciation does not necessarily adjust the recorded value of the asset to reflect the market or realisable value. An obvious example is the purchase of a motor car. As soon as the vehicle is driven away from the showroom its value falls dramatically. Another example is a piece of custom-built electronic equipment designed to test a particular product. The realisable value would be only the scrap value of the individual parts, assuming that it could not be used or adapted by another company.

It should be appreciated that the provision of depreciation as part of operating cost does not involve setting aside cash to replace the asset in due course. It is simply 'bookkeeping entries' in the financial records of the company.

Companies usually define a specific useful life to be assumed for depreciating different types of fixed assets. Typically these are:

- freehold buildings – 25 to 50 years
- plant and equipment – 5 to 20 years
- motor vehicles – 3 to 6 years.

Consider the annual depreciation charge on computer equipment which cost £140,000, where the company assumes a useful life of five years and no residual value to be realised on disposal. The annual depreciation charge will be one-fifth of the purchase price, that is £140,000 divided by 5, which is £28,000 a year.

Internal profit and loss accounts

Other terms which may occur in profit and loss accounts prepared for internal use within a company include:

- cost of sales
- gross profit
- bad debt provision.

Cost of sales

The cost of sales is more accurately described as the cost of goods and services invoiced. It is calculated as:

	£m
Value of stock and work-in-progress at beginning of financial year	430
plus	
Goods purchased and production costs incurred	2,248
less	
Value of stock and work-in-progress at end of financial year	(514)
equals	
Cost of sales	2,164

Gross profit

The gross profit is calculated as:

	£m
Sales or turnover	3,372
less	
Cost of sales	(2,164)
equals	
Gross profit	1,208

The selling and distribution costs, administration expenses and other operating costs are deducted from gross profit to calculate the operating profit.

Bad debt provision

If a customer has gone into receivership or liquidation, and there is no chance of receiving even part payment of an outstanding debt, the debt must be written off and charged to the profit and loss account.

At the end of each financial year, an estimate must be made of the eventual cost of likely bad debts as well as those actually written off. Accountants refer to these estimated amounts as provisions.

The charge to the profit and loss account each year is calculated by:

	£'000
Bad debt provision at end of year	52
plus	
Bad debt written off	17
less	69
Bad debt provision at start of year	45
Charged to profit and loss account	24

This may seem confusing, but it is not. Bad debts of £17,000 have occurred during the financial year. In addition, the estimated amount or provision for likely bad debts has been increased by £7,000 from £45,000 to £52,000. So the total charge to the profit and loss account is £17,000 plus £7,000, namely £24,000.

Dividend payment

Dividends of stockmarket-listed companies are usually paid twice a year. An interim dividend is paid after the half-year results are announced. The directors recommend a final dividend, which is paid to shareholders after they give their approval at the annual general meeting. Many private companies choose either not to pay a dividend at all, or to pay only a final dividend.

The balance sheet

The balance sheet of a company published in the Annual Report provides a financial picture of the company at the end of the financial year, showing in essence:

- the assets and liabilities of the company

and

- the sources and amounts of finance used.

('Internal' and 'external' balance sheets tend not to differ very much – additional detail may be presented on the internal balance sheet.)

It should be realised, however, that the balance sheet at the end of a financial year may give a quite different picture compared with ones prepared at other times. For example, consider a manufacturing company supplying gift items, with peak sales at Easter and Christmas. Stock levels are likely to be at their lowest in, say, February and October, when goods have been shipped to wholesalers and retailers in readiness for the selling season. The overdraft is likely to be lowest in, say, April and December, when customers have paid for their orders received in time for the peak sales periods.

Many executives find the balance sheet much harder to understand than the profit and loss account. Some give up the attempt, assuming that the balance sheet is of little importance. This is the wrong attitude. Assets must be managed as aggressively as profits, and the starting point for asset management is a thorough understanding of balance sheets.

It would be convenient if it could be safely assumed that every balance sheet has an identical format, but the reality is that balance sheet formats differ.

A simple balance sheet may have the format shown below:

Management style		*Balance sheet as at 31 March*
Fixed assets		
Tangible fixed assets		
Land and property	350	
Equipment	60	
		410
Intangible fixed assets – goodwill		110
Investment fixed assets		20
		540
Current assets	450	
Creditors: amounts falling due in less than one year within one year – (current liabilities)	(389)	
		61
Capital employed total assets less current liabilities		601
Creditors: amounts falling due after more than one year (long term liabilities)		330
Shareholders' equity		
Share capital		50
Revaluation reserve		114
Profit and loss account		107
Capital invested		601

This balances with net assets employed equalling amounts funding the business and is a sensible layout for management purposes.

Although free to balance at any line, in the UK the most common layout for statutory or published accounts is shown below. One side has net assets employed less what is owed to outsiders long-term balanced against net shareholders' investment or equity.

Fixed assets

Tangible fixed assets		
Land and property	350	
Equipment	60	
		410
Intangible fixed assets – goodwill		110
Investment fixed assets		20
		540
Current assets	450	
Creditors: amounts falling due in less than one year within one year – (current liabilities)	(389)	
		61
Capital employed total assets less current liabilities		601
Creditors: amounts falling due after more than one year (long term liabilities)		330
		271
Shareholders' equity		
Share capital		50
Revaluation reserve		114
Profit and loss account		107
Capital invested		271

Fixed assets

These include land, buildings, plant, equipment, fixtures and fittings. Fixed assets are stated at cost, less accumulated depreciation, or may be included at a professional valuation in the case of land and buildings.

Consider an asset purchased for £120,000 with an estimated useful life of five years and a residual value assessed at £20,000. The depreciation is 20 per cent a year of:

Purchase cost of £120,000

less

Estimated residual value of £20,000

equals

Depreciation of £20,000 per annum

After 3 years the net book value of the asset will be:

£'000	
Cost	120
Aggregate depreciation (3 years × 20)	60
Net book value	60

Current assets

These consist of:

- raw materials and finished goods, stocks, and work-in-progress
- debtors – amounts owed to the company by clients or customers
- deposits and short-term investments
- cash.

Creditors due within one year (current liabilities)

These consist of:

- short-term borrowings, such as overdrafts (a bank overdraft may seem a surprising item because it could be a regular feature of the balance sheet each year; this does not matter, however, since a bank overdraft is usually renegotiable annually and repayable on demand – so it is a creditor falling due within one year)
- current instalments of loans
- other creditors, such as amounts owed by the company to suppliers, shareholders (dividends) and the Inland Revenue.

Net current assets or working capital

These are current assets less creditors due within one year.

Creditors due after more than one year

These usually consist mainly of:

- secured and unsecured loans, for example a bank loan repayable after, say, four years

- obligation under finance leases for the purchase of fixed assets.

Called-up share capital

This consists of ordinary shares, and in some cases preference shares as well, both valued at nominal value. Share options are excluded until the shares are actually allotted to directors and staff. (See also share premium account below.)

Reserves

These consist of:

- retained profits

and, for example,

- share-premium account

- property revaluation reserve.

Each of these items is explained below:

1 *Retained profits*
   These are all of the profits retained in the company since its formation (after the payment of corporation tax and dividends) to provide additional finance.

2 *Share-premium account*
   This is the total of the premiums received in excess of the nominal value for all shares issued at higher than nominal value, after deducting the expenses of issuing them, for example when shares are issued as purchase consideration for an acquisition, or where additional shares are issued during the life of a company to pay for companies acquired and to raise additional capital, perhaps by way of a rights issue to existing shareholders.

   Consider a rights issue of one for two by a company with an existing issued and paid-up share capital of £300,000. The cash to be received by the company is £2.50 per share, net of expenses, compared with the nominal value of £1 per share.

- The number of shares issued will be £150,000.

- The called-up share capital will increase by £150,000 from £300,000 to £450,000.

- The cash received will be 150,000 × £2.50 = £375,000.

- The assets will increase by £375,000.

- A share premium of £225,000 will arise, that is £375,000 cash received

 less

 £150,000 additional capital issued.

This will be shown on the other side of the balance sheet under reserves.

3 *Property revaluation*
This is the increase in value over the figure included in the balance sheet arising from a professional valuation of land and buildings by a qualified property surveyor.

Real-life balance sheets often present more detailed information. A familiarity with the basic layout of a balance sheet, however, means that the detailed balance sheet is just as easy to understand. Some other items which might arise include:

Intangible assets

A small, but growing, number of companies include in the balance sheet a valuation of intangible assets (see definition earlier).

Investments

These might consist of:

- Investments in related companies, with a shareholding of between 20 and 50 per cent, which are, say, valued at the cost of the shares plus the investor company's share of retained profits and reserves since the date of acquisition.

- Investments in other companies which are valued individually at the lower of cost or net realisable value. For listed shares, net realisable value is the market value of the shares. For unlisted shares, for example in a private company, net realisable value is estimated by the directors.

Stocks

These might consist of:

- raw materials and consumables
- work-in-progress
- finished goods and goods for resale.

Stocks are valued at the lower of cost or net realisable value. Where appropriate, cost includes production and other direct overhead expenses.

Debtors

These are normally trade debtors – relating to amounts owed by customers.

Other creditors (due within one year)

These can consist of:

- trade creditors – relating to amounts owed to suppliers
- corporation taxation
- ordinary dividend payable
- current-year obligations under finance leases for the purchase of assets.

Provisions for liabilities and charges

Obligations such as payments to the staff pension scheme and deferred taxation.

Special reserve

This is an item not commonly encountered. It might be described as a technical adjustment to the balance sheet. It could arise where the share-premium account has been reduced by a transfer to an non-distributable special reserve, following a special resolution passed by shareholders and confirmed by court order.

Related companies' reserves

A group's share of the reserves of related companies.

Minority shareholders' interests

The value of that part of subsidiary companies owned by minority shareholders directly in the subsidiary, rather than by a group.

Goodwill

Goodwill merits an explanation. On the acquisition of a business, where the price paid exceeds the value of the net assets acquired, the difference is treated as goodwill. Companies used to write off goodwill against the reserves in the year of acquisition and so it did not appear on the balance sheet. Contemporary standard accounting practice is to capitalise it on the balance sheet and review its worth annually for 'impairment' – that is, loss in value. Any loss in value has to be written off through the profit and loss account as an exceptional item.

Research and development

Research and development is an item which occurs infrequently on a balance sheet, because most companies write off the expenditure in the year in which it is incurred as a charge to the profit and loss account, rather than capitalise it as an asset on the balance sheet.

Cash flow statement

Companies are required to publish a cash flow statement annually, in addition to a profit and loss account and balance sheet.

The cash flow statement shows cash flows from:

- operating activities
- dividends from joint ventures and associates
- returns on investments and servicing of finance
- taxation
- capital expenditure and financial investment
- acquisitions and disposals
- equity dividends paid
- management of liquid resources
- financing.

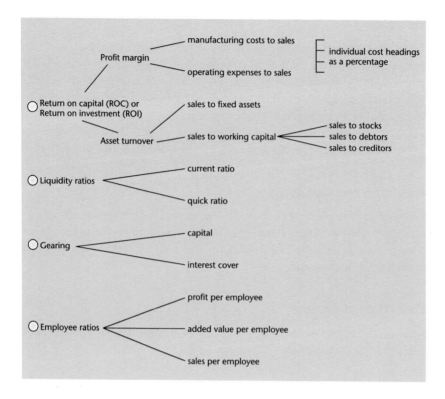

An understanding of the flow of cash in and out of a business is essential. There may be earnings and profits, but is there cash?

Ratio analysis

The range of ratio analyses and their uses are examined under the headings Performance ratios and Stockmarket ratios.

Performance ratios

These ratios can be broken down as follows:

Some business executives regard ratio analysis as the preserve of accountants. Nothing could be more wrong. Ratio analysis is an essential tool for managers. It can indicate the extent of the financial well-being of a business or give an early warning of an unsatisfactory trend. Ratio analysis can be used to:

- assess the current performance of a business, on a monthly basis
- evaluate the acceptability of the budget proposed for the next financial year

- compare performance of subsidiaries and divisions within a group
- compare performance with that achieved by competitors, on an annual basis.

The first step is to define the various ratios used to evaluate business performance and to understand their significance.

Return on investment

The key yardstick of financial performance within a business is the return on investment achieved, and it is usually measured annually.

The basic definition is simple:

Per cent return on investment =

$$\frac{\text{Profit} - (\times\ 100)}{\text{The amount invested to produce the profit}}$$

(Sometimes ROI is used as an abbreviation for return on investment.)

What happens in practice can be thoroughly confusing to non-accountants.

Different definitions of profit and investment are used by different companies, and as a result different terms may be encountered such as 'return on capital employed' (ROCE) and 'return on operating assets' (ROA).

Fortunately, there is an easy way to cut through this confusion: ask one of the finance staff in your company to explain the definition they have adopted. Some accountants will debate the merits of their particular definition at length. When used to evaluate performance within a group or company, however, the most important features are that the definition adopted is:

- easily understood by both managers and finance staff
- used in a consistent way by each division and subsidiary.

This is because there is no consensus among qualified accountants on a correct definition of return on investment.

Nonetheless, it is helpful to know the definitions most commonly used for profit and investment in connection with return on investment.

Profit is usually defined as either profit before interest and tax or as profit before tax.

Investment may be defined as:

- the capital employed as shown on the balance sheet, namely the fixed and current assets employed in the business minus all of the liabilities, or

- the operating assets employed, namely fixed assets, plus current assets, less creditors due within one year, excluding bank overdrafts and other borrowings.

Clearly, the percentage return on investment figures calculated for a particular company may differ significantly depending upon the definitions chosen for profit and investment. For the purpose of comparison within a company, however, it is worth stressing that it is the changes and differences in the ratios which are of prime importance.

Freehold land and building valuation

In the balance sheet of a listed company, the valuation of freehold land and buildings will probably be updated at least every five years, in order to avoid a significant understatement of asset values. For a private company, if the freehold property is not needed as security for bank loans, the valuation in the balance sheet may be left at the original purchase cost of, say, 20 or more years ago. The only reference to this undervaluation in the Annual Report may be an item in the Directors' Report stating that the current market value is greater than the figure shown in the balance sheet.

By calculating a return on investment on this undervalued freehold basis, however, the owners may be fooling themselves that the return on investment is satisfactory when it is not. Consider the following example:

Per cent return on operating assets (ROA)

$$= \frac{\text{Profit before interest and tax}}{\text{Operating assets employed}}$$

$$= \frac{\text{say, £264,000}}{\text{£1.2m}}$$

= 22 per cent, based on balance sheet valuation

If the value of the freehold property is understated by, say, £800,000, then on a current-valuation basis:

Per cent return on operating assets (ROA) =

$$= \frac{\text{£264,000}}{\text{£1.2m + £0.8m}}$$

= 13.2 per cent, based on current freehold valuation

Acceptable level of return on investment

It is a step forward to understand the calculation of return on investment, but this does not answer the important question: 'What is an acceptable percentage return?'

Clearly the percentage return on investment should exceed:

- the percentage return achievable from a relatively risk-free investment, such as a major building society, expressed grossed up for income tax at the standard rate – because otherwise a better return could be achieved simply by investing the money and receiving the interest

- the cost of overdraft interest – because otherwise the return achieved does not cover the borrowing cost of the investment.

In practice, however, an acceptable return on investment should be significantly higher than the above to provide an adequate reward for the risks involved and the management expertise required.

Many stockmarket-listed companies regard an acceptable return on operating assets, calculated using profit before interest and tax, to be a minimum of 20 per cent. More importantly, however, these companies would regard 25 per cent as a realistic goal to be achieved.

An analysis of return on investment

To manage the return on investment may seem to call for the ability to juggle simultaneously two completely different aspects of a business: profit and the funds invested. What is more, it may appear just as difficult to do as juggling not two, but seven balls at once.

Fortunately, return on investment can be broken down into two separate and more easily manageable aspects of business:

Return on investment

$$= \frac{\text{Profit before tax and interest}}{\text{Assets employed}}$$

$$= \frac{\text{Profit before tax and interest}}{\substack{\text{Sales turnover} \\ \text{(or fee income)}}} \times \frac{\text{Sales turnover}}{\substack{\text{Assets} \\ \text{employed}}}$$

$$= \text{Per cent profit margin on sales} \times \text{Assets turnover}$$

So the key to improving the return on investment is to increase:

- either the per cent profit margin on sales

- or the asset turnover

- or, better still, both of these.

To do any of these may seem almost as daunting as the apparent juggling needed to improve the return on investment. This is not so. Both the profit margin on sales and the asset turnover can be broken down into more easily manageable parts.

Profit margin on sales

The items which determine the per cent profit margin on sales are:

Sales turnover or fee income

less

Cost of sales

equals

Gross profit

less

departmental overhead costs, including depreciation charges where these occur (e.g. marketing, sales, research and development, production, distribution, finance, administration)

equals

Profit before interest and tax.

Profit before interest and tax

So it becomes obvious that effective management and control of the percentage profit margin on sales require attention to:

- the percentage gross profit achieved, namely gross profit expressed as a percentage of sales turnover, and

- the percentage of departmental costs, namely departmental costs expressed as a percentage of sales turnover.

The percentage profit before interest and tax on sales turnover tends to vary widely with the nature of the business. For construction companies it may be as low as between 2 and 4 per cent. For food supermarkets and some wholesale businesses it may be between 3 and 5 per cent. At the other extreme, some service companies may achieve more than 15 per cent. Many businesses achieve less than 10 per cent profit before interest and tax on sales turnover.

So every decimal point of percentage profit margin is important. For example, consider a business with an annual sales turnover of £10m and the following budgeted costs for the year ahead:

Year ahead Budget	£m	%
Sales turnover	10.00	100.0
Cost of sales	3.88	38.8
Gross profit	6.12	61.2
Marketing	0.63	6.3
Sales and customer service	2.37	23.7
Distribution	0.90	9.0
Development	0.93	9.3
Finance and administration	0.47	4.7
Profit before interest and tax	0.82	8.2

During the year assume that the gross profit falls from 61.2 to 60.3 per cent, a decrease of only 0.9 percentage points. One response is to regard a gross profit of more than 60 per cent as a figure that many businesses would envy. This would be totally unacceptable to the profit-driven manager. Assuming that departmental overhead costs remain the same percentage of turnover as budgeted, this means that the profit margin will fall from 8.2 to 7.3 per cent, a similar decrease of 0.9 percentage points. On a sales turnover of £10m, the profit before interest and tax will fall by £90,000, from £820,000 to £730,000.

Now consider a situation where:

- the actual sales turnover falls to £9.5m compared with budgeted sales of £10m

- the cost of sales remains at the budgeted level of 38.8 per cent

- total overheads are allowed to remain at the budgeted amount of £5.3m.

Whereas the total overheads were budgeted to be 53 per cent of sales turnover, if the overheads remain at £5.3m, these become 55.8 per cent of the reduced sales turnover of £9.5m. So the profit margin will fall by a similar amount from 8.2 to 5.4 per cent, because overheads have increased by 2.8 percentage points. Profit before interest and tax will fall from £820,000 to £540,000.

The message is clear. When sales turnover falls, every effort must be made to reduce overhead levels as much as possible to offset partially the loss of profit, while avoiding lasting damage to the infrastructure of the business.

Asset turnover

For many managers, the concept of managing asset turnover is likely to be less familiar than that of managing the profit margin on sales. It makes the point, however, that every pound's worth of assets invested in the business must be made to work, or better still to 'sweat', to achieve the highest possible level of sales.

What does this mean in practical terms? Consider a hotel with a ballroom that is used only in the evening for dinner dances and banquets. A relatively modest investment in moveable partitions may allow the room to be used for conferences of various sizes during the day. The introduction of either a 'twilight shift' in the evenings or a seven-days-a-week 'continental shift' may allow increased sales and asset turnover to be achieved from expensive production facilities. Equally, when new expenditure is being made on equipping a new retail sales unit or installing costly production equipment, speed is essential. The aim must be to bring the facilities into use as soon as possible in order to increase asset turnover. Unused floor space, whether owned or rented, is costly. The action to be taken will depend upon how long the space is likely to remain unused. It may include subletting unused space on a short-term basis or relocating part of the business to allow a complete building to be let or sold.

Working capital must be used just as productively as investment in fixed assets. The main elements of working capital are stock and work-in-progress, and debtors (cash owed to the business by customers) and creditors (cash owed by the business). Some managers believe that stock and work-in-progress levels, debtors and creditors are the responsibility of the finance function. This is nonsense. Managers must exercise their accountability to manage these elements of working capital with the assistance of finance staff.

Separate ratios need to be calculated for:

* stock and work-in-progress
* debtors
* creditors.

Each one is defined and explained as follows:

Stock ratios

Stock ratios are usually expressed in one of two ways:

* the number of days of stock and work-in-progress held, or
* the number of times stock and work-in-progress is turned over annually.

The calculations are:

$$\text{Stock turnover (days)} =$$

$$\frac{\text{Average stock and work-in-progress during year}}{\text{Annual cost of sales}} \times 365$$

$$\text{(Annual) stock turnover} = \frac{\text{Annual cost of sales}}{\text{Average stock and work-in-progress during year}}$$

It may seem surprising that the annual cost of sales is used to calculate stock turnover rather than annual sales. The reason is simply to compare like with like, because stock values and cost of sales are calculated on the same basis.

Consider the following example:

	£m
Annual sales	10.00
Cost of sales	3.88
Gross profit	6.12
Stock and work-in-progress:	
at beginning of year	1.87
at end of year	2.21
Average stock and work-in-progress	2.04

$$\text{Stock turnover (days)}$$

$$= \frac{\text{Average stock and work-in-progress}}{\text{Annual cost of sales}}$$

$$= \frac{£2.04m}{£3.88m} \times 365 = 192 \text{ days}$$

$$\text{(Annual) stock turnover}$$

$$= \frac{\text{Annual cost of sales}}{\text{Average stock and work-in-progress}}$$

$$= \frac{£3.88m}{£2.04m} = 1.9 \text{ times}$$

Of the two methods commonly used, the stock turnover in days is probably more meaningful for managers. If in the following year the value of stock and work-in-progress were to increase from 192 days to, say, 199 days, it is obvious that it has taken an extra week to turn inventory into sales. The corresponding change in annual stock turnover from 1.9 times to 1.83 times is less revealing.

In a manufacturing company with a large investment in inventory, it may make sense to calculate separate ratios for:

- raw materials
- work-in-progress
- finished goods ready for sale

in order to identify where corrective action is most needed.

Debtor ratio

On an annual basis, this is usually calculated by:

$$\text{Debtor ratio} = \frac{\text{Debtors at year end}}{\text{Annual sales}} \times 365 \text{ (number of debtor days)}$$

On a monthly basis, this is often calculated on an equivalent number of days. For example, consider this calculation of the debtor ratio for June:

Value of outstanding debtors
at end of June = £130,000

Invoiced sales – June = £57,000
– May = £63,000
– April = £50,000

Outstanding debtors of £130,000 is equivalent to sales in:

June of £57,000 = 30 days
May of £63,000 = 31 days
April of £10,000 = 6 days (pro rata to month of sales of £50,000)
Total = 67 days

Every business, regardless of size, should monitor the number of debtor days outstanding each month. An increase of only a single day during a month requires immediate corrective action. Consider the impact of an increase in debtor days outstanding for a relatively small business with an annual sales turnover of £3.65m, namely £10,000 a calendar day. Assume that the average number of debtor days is allowed to increase by seven days throughout the financial year, that is, customers are allowed an extra week to pay their invoices. The effect is significant on both the bank overdraft and the amount of profit:

- the bank overdraft will increase by £70,000 (because an extra seven days' sales, at £10,000 per day, will remain unpaid)
- the additional overdraft interest on additional borrowings of £70,000 for a year at, say, 14 per cent interest, will be almost £10,000 a year.

In a business with significant export sales, which may take considerably longer to be paid for, there is a case for calculating the debtor days separately for each month:

- home sales
- export sales
- total sales.

Creditor ratio

On an annual basis, this is usually calculated by:

Creditor ratio

$$\frac{\text{Creditors at year end}}{\text{Annual purchases}} \times 365$$

= no. of creditor days

On a monthly basis, this is often calculated on the basis of an equivalent number of days, in the same way as for debtors. Knowing the number of days of credit being taken from suppliers, enables a manager to ensure that the policy of payment to suppliers is being adhered to, in overall terms.

Liquidity ratios

The survival of a business depends upon the ability to pay creditors acceptably soon enough. Liquidity ratios indicate the ability to pay creditors due within one year sufficiently quickly. There are two types:

- current ratio
- quick ratio.

Current ratio

A commonly used definition is:

$$\text{Current ratio} = \frac{\text{Current assets}}{\text{Creditors due within a year, excluding borrowings}}$$

Current assets are primarily stocks, work-in-progress, debtors, cash-in-hand and any other liquid resources. The current assets represent the cash – which is constantly circulating – tied up in the business. In a manufacturing company, raw materials are purchased, then pass through the work-in-progress stage during the production process, become finished goods (stock for sale), are turned into debtors when the sale is invoiced and finally produce cash when the customer pays. The cycle starts again when some of the cash is used to purchase more raw materials.

Clearly, the current assets should comfortably exceed the value of creditors due for payment within a year to ensure that invoices can be paid sufficiently promptly. If the current assets were only to equal the creditors due within a year, then some increase in borrowing would probably be needed, simply because some of the current assets would be tied up in stocks and work-in-progress and so would take longer to be turned into cash.

One rule of thumb is that the current ratio of a healthy business should be at least 2.0, in order to provide an adequate safety margin to ensure that invoices can be paid sufficiently quickly. It has to be said, however, that many large and successful companies, with adequate unused borrowing facilities, operate on a current ratio much nearer to 1.0 than 2.0.

Quick ratio

A commonly used definition is:

$$\text{Quick ratio} = \frac{\text{Current assets, excluding stock and work-in-progress}}{\text{Creditors due within one year}}$$

This means that the 'cash and near-cash' resources – debtors, cash-in-hand and any other liquid assets – are being compared with outstanding invoices which need to be paid.

If the ratio is less than 1.0, the implications may be that:

- additional borrowings will be needed to pay creditors sufficiently quickly

- extended credit will have to be taken, with the likelihood of court action for non-payment of invoices and the withholding of deliveries by suppliers

- the business requires an injection of capital to finance the present scale of operations adequately.

Nonetheless, some businesses do manage to survive for a surprisingly long time with a quick ratio significantly below 1.0. It has to be said, however, that the important word is 'survive'. Such a warning signal should not be ignored.

Gearing ratio

The gearing ratio shows the percentage of borrowed money in relation to the shareholders' funds in the company. A commonly used definition is:

$$\text{Gearing ratio} = \frac{\text{Net borrowings}}{\text{Shareholders' funds}} \times 100 \text{ per cent}$$

(= percentage gearing)

Net borrowings are bank loans and overdrafts minus cash-in-hand and other liquid resources.

Shareholders' funds are represented by the balance-sheet valuation of the shareholders' funds invested in the company. These are then issued as paid-up share capital, at nominal value, plus accumulated reserves. The reserves are the profit retained in the business since it was formed, plus any property-revaluation surplus and share-premium account value where appropriate.

These are occasions when even companies listed on a stockmarket have a gearing ratio in excess of 100 per cent. This means that lenders are providing more finance to operate the business than the shareholders. Indeed, there have been notable instances where listed companies have – temporarily – had a gearing ratio in the region of 250 per cent. This may have been the result of a large amount of borrowing to pay for a major acquisition. In these circumstances, however, it is likely that the chairman's statement in the Annual Report will state what has already been done, and what more will be done, to reduce the level of gearing substantially. Indeed, it may be necessary to sell some businesses in order to reduce the gearing sufficiently quickly to an acceptable level.

The consequence of a high gearing ratio is a heavy burden of loan and overdraft interest charged to the profit and loss account. When the economic climate deteriorates, there may well be a compound effect on profit. Not only are trading profits likely to fall, but interest rates could increase as well.

One way of calculating the effect of gearing upon profit is to calculate the interest cover, which is commonly defined as:

$$\text{Interest cover} = \frac{\text{Profit before interest and tax (number of times)}}{\text{Interest payable}}$$

A rule of thumb, which should not be ignored because the cost may be a loss of financial prudence, is that the interest cover should be at least 4.0 and preferably 5.0 or more using the above definition.

Employee ratios

Some businesses use various employee ratios as a measure of productivity, especially during periods of rapid expansion when productivity may fall in the pursuit of growth. Commonly used ratios include:

- *sales per employee* – but this could be maintained or increased as a result of a higher 'bought-in material' or 'subcontracted' content of sales

- *added value per employee* – added value eliminates the possible distortion of any differences in the bought-in and subcontracted content by deducting these from sales

- *profit before tax per employee* – which can be highly revealing.

In professional partnerships, useful employee ratios include:

- average fee income per professional staff person

- average fee income per equity partner

- average profit before tax per equity partner.

For example, consider a professional partnership with:

Annual fee income	= £5.61m
Total fee earners	= 50
Number of equity partners	= 10
Profit before tax	= £960,000
Average fee per fee earner	= £112,000 (£5.6m/50)
Average fee income per equity partner	= £560,000 (£5.6m/10)
Average profit before tax per equity partner	= £96,000 (960,000/10)

Another useful ratio to use in a professional partnership is the professional staff support ratio, defined as:

$$\text{Professional staff support ratio} = \frac{\text{Total number of professional staff}}{\text{Total number of other staff}}$$

To maintain profitability, any increase in this ratio must be adequately justified and not allowed to happen by accident or indulgence.

Indexation

When analysing trends in the performance of a company over five years or more, inflation of even 5–10 per cent a year distorts the picture significantly. One method of analysis is to index the figures using a base of 100 for the first year, then to adjust subsequent years' figures using the movement in the appropriate index, such as the retail price index.

Using ratio analysis

Some managers want to know what is a 'good' or 'correct' figure for a particular ratio. This misses the point of ratio analysis. For example, a 'nil' gearing ratio (indicating no borrowings at all) could be 'bad' rather than 'good'. It could reflect the fact that profitable opportunities have not been pursued because of an excessively conservative dislike of borrowing.

As noted earlier, some ratios differ widely according to the nature of the industry. Generally, profit margins in the construction industry are likely to be dramatically lower than those of companies supplying luxury goods. Within a particular company, the trends are of most importance. For example, ratio analysis reveals whether productivity and profitability are declining in the pursuit of rapid growth.

Comparisons with competitors

Ratio analysis provides the opportunity to compare the performance of a company with that of competitors. Simply to obtain a copy of the published accounts of competitors and to calculate the ratios may produce some surprising contrasts and some equally misleading figures because:

- profit may be calculated on a different basis
- balance sheets may be valued on a different basis.

Some examples will make the point emphatically. Consider the treatment of methods and rates of depreciation.

There can be significant differences in balance-sheet treatment. A company may have revalued property assets this year. A competitor may not have revalued property for four years. The accounting rules allow brand names which are purchased, but not those created by a company, to be valued in the balance sheet. A small but growing number of companies now include a valuation of brand names purchased as part of a company acquisition in their balance sheets.

Generally, an experienced accountant is needed to 'guesstimate' the various adjustments required in published accounts for any worthwhile comparisons and conclusions to be made. Recognising this difficulty, members of some trade associations submit their results in a standardised format to a major firm of chartered accountants so that ratios can be circulated to the participants anonymously. Another source of useful information may be an intercompany ratio comparison in selected business sectors available from a commercial publisher.

Stockmarket ratios

These can be broken down as follows:

- gross dividend yield
- dividend cover
- earnings per share
- price-earnings ratio
- market capitalisation
- net asset backing.

It would be understandable for people working in a subsidiary or a division of a stockmarket-listed company to consider that stockmarket ratios were irrelevant to their job. The owner of a private company may take a similar view. Both would be wrong, for different reasons.

People working in stockmarket-listed companies need to know the yardsticks by which the performance of their company is judged, and the consequences for inadequate results, namely the real threat of being taken over and the risk of substantial job losses.

For owners of private companies, a knowledge of stockmarket ratios is needed to understand the performance required if they decide to obtain a stockmarket listing, or to take a realistic view of the amount an acquirer may pay to purchase the company.

At first sight, even the names of the various ratios seem complicated and daunting: gross dividend yield, dividend cover, earnings per share, price earnings ratio, market capitalisation and net asset backing per share sound like a foreign language. The reality is totally different. Once explained these ratios are simple to understand and calculate. Each ratio will now be defined in turn, and then a worked example used to illustrate the calculation.

Gross dividend yield

The gross dividend yield is the return received by the shareholder through the receipt of a dividend, ignoring any deduction of income tax, calculated as a percentage of the current market price of the shares. The method of calculation is:

$$\text{Gross dividend yield} = \frac{\text{Gross annual dividend per share (before deduction of income tax)}}{\text{Current market share price}}$$

This is a different calculation from that for the gross percentage dividend, which is:

$$\text{Gross percentage dividend} = \frac{\text{Gross annual dividend per share}}{\text{Nominal value of share}}$$

An understandable reaction would be: why bother with an extra calculation? The answer is simple. The percentage dividend allows comparison only with the dividend paid by the same company in previous years. The gross dividend yield allows a meaningful comparison to be made of the relative dividend income to be received from the shares of different companies.

Dividend cover

The dividend cover is the number of times the profits, after tax earned for the ordinary shareholders, exceed or 'cover' the gross dividend paid. The method of calculation is:

$$\text{Dividend cover} = \frac{\text{Earnings}}{\text{Gross dividend paid}}$$

The word 'earnings' is shorthand for the profits after tax earned for the ordinary shareholder in the parent company, before deducting extraordinary items.

The dividend cover may be regarded as an indication of the safety margin by which the earnings exceed the gross dividend. If the dividend cover is 1.0, this means that all the earnings, namely profits after tax, have been used to pay the dividend to shareholders. If the dividend cover is less than 1.0, which sometimes happens, in effect the shareholders are being paid some of the capital value of their share disguised as a dividend. Maintaining the same dividend payment in pence per share as was made in the previous year may be a conscious decision by the board, faced with a disappointing profit for the year, as a show of confidence. The message behind this decision is: 'Don't worry; the setback will not be repeated next year.' What it does mean, however, is that the company may have had to increase its overdraft to maintain the dividend payment, and so has to start the financial year with the prospect of an increased interest charge to the profit and loss account.

The most important source of finance for any company is profit retained in the business, after paying corporation tax and an acceptable level of dividend to shareholders. A stockmarket-listed company should aim to pay an adequate dividend yield and still be able to achieve a dividend cover greater than 2.0; that is, more profit should be left in the company to finance business development and growth than is paid to shareholders by dividend.

Earnings per share

The earnings per share is expressed in pence, and is the earnings for the year divided by the weighted average number of shares in issue during the year. The method of calculation is:

Earnings per share =

$$\frac{\text{Earnings}}{\text{Weighted average number of issued shares}} \times 100 \text{ (pence per share)}$$

A key measure of profitability for a stockmarket-listed company is the growth in earnings per share, because it takes into account not merely trading profit from operations, but also the effect of interest charges on profit and the overall level of corporation tax. Thus the earnings are the total income earned from shareholders, not just the amount of dividend paid, together with the ability to raise finance without issuing more ordinary shares.

Whenever additional shares are issued, for example:

- to finance expansion through a rights issue (see below) to existing shareholders

- to pay for the acquisition of another company, instead of using cash

- to executives under a share-option scheme

then the weighted average number of share issued increases, and unless the earnings increase by a similar proportion, the earnings per share will be reduced. The expression often used to describe this situation is 'a dilution in the earnings per share'.

A rights issue is an issue of shares for cash made to existing shareholders, pro rata to their existing holding of shares. For example, a 1 for 4 rights issue means that each shareholder is entitled to buy one additional share for every four already owned. In the case of a listed company, the shareholder has the opportunity to sell the rights rather than buy the additional shares, and will receive any surplus value of the market price for the shares compared with the rights-issue price.

The aim of a stockmarket-listed company should be to maximise the growth in earnings per share through the medium and long term, without a reduction or setback in any year. The most successful listed companies have achieved compound annual growth in earnings per share of more than 20 per cent a year over a decade and longer.

Price-earnings ratio

Price-earning ratios, often referred to as PE ratios, for stockmarket-listed companies are published daily in the *Financial Times*, along with the gross dividend yield, dividend cover and other information about the shares of each company. The method of calculation is what the name suggests:

$$\text{Price-earnings ratio} = \frac{\text{Stockmarket share price}}{\text{Earnings per share}}$$

The stockmarket share price used is the one published in the financial newspapers at the close of business in the stock exchange the previous evening.

If, say, the average price-earnings ratio of a cross-section of several hundred companies was 12.9, this could be interpreted to mean that the share price of a typical company was 12.9 times the earnings per share achieved in the previous year.

In general, when the price-earnings ratio of a company is higher than the average for other companies in the same business sector, the stockmarket expects the company to achieve higher than average earnings per share in the foreseeable future to justify the above-average valuation of the shares. In some circumstances, the explanation may be quite different. For example, a takeover bid for the company may be widely expected, and the share price has already increased significantly in anticipation of the price to be offered by the bidder.

It must never be forgotten that the analysis of share prices, and especially the prediction of future changes, cannot be done simply by calculating the various ratios. If this was possible, making a fortune on the stockmarket would be easy. In practice, even the most experienced investment-fund managers make costly errors of judgement from time to time.

(Note: EBITDA [Earnings before Interest, taxes, Depreciation, Amortisation] can be used with or instead of the P/E ratio but is a crude valuation multiple in many circumstances.)

Market capitalisation

The market capitalisation of a stockmarket-listed company is simply the total value placed upon the shares of the company. It is calculated by:

Market capitalisation = number of issued shares × most recent share price

Of course, the market capitalisation does not indicate the price a takeover bidder would have to pay to acquire the company. Typically, even if a rival bidder does not make an increased bid, an offer of about 35 per cent more than the share price when the offer was first anticipated may be needed for a successful bid. In a contested takeover, a successful bid may need to be at least 50 per cent more than the previous price of the shares.

Net asset backing

The net asset backing is usually expressed in pence per share and is the balance-sheet worth of each share. It is calculated by.

$$\text{Net asset backing} = \frac{\text{Shareholders' funds in the balance sheet (price per share)}}{\text{Number of issued shares}}$$

The shareholders' funds consist of the issued share capital, calculated at the nominal value, plus reserves. In addition to retained profits, the reserves include the share-premium account and any property revaluation where appropriate.

Some people find it surprising that the net asset backing per share shown by the audited balance sheet of a company may be significantly higher or lower than the present market price of the shares. Once again, the reason is simple. For most companies, the prime determinants of the market share price are the most recent earnings per share and the expected future growth. Balance-sheet asset values tend to have a major influence on the share price only when a substantial proportion of the share price is in the form of available cash within the company and readily saleable freehold properties.

For a profitable company which is not capital intensive, such as a successful advertising agency, the net asset backing per share may be only a small proportion of the market price of the shares. In contrast, consider a manufacturing company with poor profitability and high asset backing per share in the balance sheet. The likelihood is that the assets could not be turned into a corresponding amount of cash, even by liquidating the company. So the market share price will be depressed by the poor profitability, and may well be significantly lower than the net asset backing per share shown by the balance sheet.

Worked example

Consider the share information for a (fictional) company that might appear in the *Financial Times*:

Year in question					*Div.*		*Yield*	
High	*Low*	*Stock*	*Price* +	*or* –	*Net*	*Cover*	*Gross*	*P/E*
595	425	Hickbush Holdings 50p 558		-4	15.0	2.4	3.6	11.6

The information tells you that the:

- highest market share price to date in year was 595p

- lowest market share price was 425p

- nominal value of each share is 50p

- share price at the close of business last evening was 558p (the average of the buying and selling prices)

- (average) share price was 4p lower than the previous evening

- total dividend paid on each share in the previous finance year was 15.0p, after the deduction of income tax at the standard rate of 25 per cent

- dividend cover in the previous year was 2.4 times the amount of dividend paid

- gross dividend yield in the previous year was 3.6 per cent

- price-earnings ratio is 11.6 at the most recent share price of 558p.

The calculation of the stockmarket ratios for this fictional company would be based on the above data and on the following information taken from its Annual Report:

- gross dividend per share: 20p

- earnings: £412.0m

- gross dividend paid: £172.1m

- number of issued shares: 860.6m

- shareholders' funds in balance sheet: £3,438m.

Gross dividend yield
(the percentage of current share
price the investor receives as
dividend)

$$= \frac{\text{Gross dividend per share}}{\text{Market share price}}$$

$$= \frac{20.0p}{558p}$$

= **3.6 per cent**

Dividend cover
(the number of times the
profit attributable to the
ordinary shareholder covers
the dividend for the year)

$$\frac{\text{Earnings}}{\text{Gross dividend paid}}$$

$$= \frac{£412.0m}{£172.1m}$$

= **2.4 times**

Earnings per share
(the profit attributable
to the ordinary shareholder
earned in pence
per share)

$$\frac{\text{Earnings}}{\text{Weighted average number of issued shares}}$$

$$= \frac{£412.0m}{860.6m}$$

= **48p per share**

Price-earnings ratio
(the number of years
required at last year's
earnings to equal the
market price of the share)

$$= \frac{\text{Stockmarket share price}}{\text{Earnings per share}}$$

$$= \frac{558p}{48p}$$

= 11.6

Market capitalisation
(the aggregate value of the
ordinary shares at the
present market share price)

= Number of shares issued at
year end × market share price
= 860.6m × 558p
= £4.8 billion

Net asset backing per share
(value of shareholders' funds
per ordinary share as show•
in the balance sheet)

$$= \frac{\text{Shareholders' funds in balance sheet}}{\text{Number of issued shares}}$$

$$= \frac{£3,438m}{860.6m}$$

= **399p per share**

Comparative share performance

Occasionally, someone will ask 'What is a good price-earnings ratio?', implying that there is a universal and everlasting benchmark to aim for. This misses the point completely. Consider the sharp falls in share prices that occur from time to time and affect stockmarkets in many countries. When share prices fall by more than 20 per cent in many cases, it means that price-earnings (PE) ratios fall by a similar percentage, as the PE ratio is calculated by dividing the most recent share price by the earnings per share. At any time, average PE ratios can differ significantly among the stockmarkets of different countries. Equally, the PE ratios for different types of business on the same stockmarket can vary widely.

The FT-Actuaries Share Indices table, published daily by the *Financial Times*, gives the PE ratios and gross dividend yields for a variety of business sectors.

The most relevant comparisons to make for the shares of a particular company are with:

- the sector average in the FT-Actuaries Share Indices table
- broadly similar companies.

Share value in private companies

Owners of private companies sometimes have extravagant and quite unrealistic views about the worth of their business if it were to be sold. The use of PE ratios gives a broad indication of the possible price an acquirer may be prepared to pay.

Consider a privately owned building materials company. Assume the profits before tax in a year were £600,000, and an increase to £650,000 is forecast for the following year. The net assets of the business, taking into account the present value of the freehold property, is £2.4m. The owners believe the business is worth at least £5m.

Valuation of private companies using PE ratios is usually done on the assumption that a full 27 per cent corporation tax should be deducted from the profits before tax to calculate the earnings.

Actual profit before tax	£600,000
Less, say, 27 per cent tax	(£162,000)
Earnings	£438,000

Say the PE ratio of the building materials sector was 10.8. The forecast profit growth for the following year is roughly 'average', so it could be assumed that the average PE ratio would be used by a takeover bidder. Wrong! The evidence is that many buyers of private companies look for a discount on a comparable PE ratio for stockmarket-listed companies of at least 20 per cent. This would suggest a PE ratio of about 8.6 times the earnings of £438,000, which is less than £3.8m. It must be stressed, however, that PE ratios give only a broad indication of the likely purchase price for a private company. Factors which may increase the purchase price include:

- scarcity or rarity value, resulting from a shortage of attractive companies available to purchase in the sector
- being a market leader in a niche business
- additional profit opportunities to be gained by the acquirer.

Factors which are likely to reduce the purchase price include:

- undue dependence on one customer
- low asset backing relative to the purchase price
- particular reliance on the personal contribution of the present owners, which may be difficult to replace.

Techniques to increase profits

The main techniques examined are:

- budgetary control
- cash management
- profit management
- financial analysis for decision-making.

Budgetary control

Sound budgets, prompt monthly reporting of actual results, and a regularly updated forecast of the results expected for the financial year are the essential foundations of financial management control.

Basic issues

First-class procedures are not sufficient to ensure effective budgeting and budgetary control. Suitable management attitudes are essential. These require two basic issues to be addressed:

1 What level of achievement should the budget reflect?
2 Who is responsible for achieving budgeted performance?

The budgeted level of performance should be demanding, but achievable by committed and co-ordinated management action.

It is not enough for the managing director, general manager, or a regional manager in charge of a separate business to be committed to the achievement of the budgeted profit. Nothing less than the collective commitment of the person in charge and each member of the team reporting directly to him or her is acceptable. Otherwise, people may adopt the parochial view that their only responsibility and concern is to achieve the sales or control the costs in line with their departmental budget. This would be nonsense, and must not be allowed to happen. For example, if the gross profit from sales falls below budget, every effort must be made to offset this by appropriate cost reduction throughout the business.

Budget assumptions

The assumptions on which the budget is to be constructed should be agreed by the executive team and written down at the outset, to ensure that different departments do not make different assumptions and that the proposed budget can be reviewed by top management for changes required. Assumptions which need to be made and written down include:

- price increases for existing products and services
  - the proposed percentage increase and date to be implemented for each product or service group
- the date for the launch of each new product or service
- the dates planned for other events which will affect the budget such as:
  - new branch or store openings
  - relocation of premises
  - the appointment of additional distributors
- expected salary increases
- cost inflation for the various categories of expenditure
- currency exchange rates and commodity price movements, where appropriate
- the recruitment of additional staff
- major items of discretionary expenses within departmental budgets, such as marketing or research and development
- substantial capital expenditure projects

- impact of anticipated legislation and other external factors such as:
  - higher national insurance contributions
  - additional costs arising from, for example, new requirements on food packaging.

Co-ordination

Most businesses are organised into numerous separate departments and functions. If detailed budgets are prepared by each department and then simply aggregated into an overall budget for the business, the resulting profit and cash flow may be unacceptable. Co-ordination at an early stage is needed to ensure this does not happen. An effective way to achieve this co-ordination is by the executive directors of the business collectively preparing and agreeing an acceptable outline budget before the preparation of detailed departmental budgets is started. The outline budget needs to be no more than an outline profit and loss and cash flow budget for the year. It means, however, that each director will know what departmental budget will be acceptable from the outset.

Sales budget

Ideally, the sales budget will be prepared and the implications for other departments discussed with them before they need to start preparing their detailed budgets. Otherwise, departments such as purchasing, production, order processing and physical distribution will have to base their budgets upon a 'guesstimate' of the volume and mix of sales to be budgeted.

Every effort must be made to budget sales as accurately as possible, despite the uncertainties involved. Any variance between budgeted and actual sales is likely to have a disproportionately greater effect on budgeted profit and cash flow.

Sales value should not merely be estimated as a total amount, but should be calculated from the number of units to be sold and the sales prices to be obtained.

Overhead costs

The annual budgeting exercise provides an opportunity not merely to budget departmental costs for the coming year but also to challenge the existence, size and methods of each department. Unfortunately, not enough companies seize this opportunity.

It may sound like a recipe for anarchy, but it is not. The technique is known as zero-based budgeting and variations of it have been used for many years by some companies. In essence, it means adopting a blank piece of paper approach by considering how the need would best be served if the department did not exist. For example, perhaps physical distribution of goods could be subcontracted out completely rather than provided by company-owned vehicles with a large number of staff employed. Or at least vehicles could be leased instead of owned. The real benefits to be gained from zero-based budgeting arise from thinking about and challenging existing methods and standards.

Staff salaries, and the costs which inevitably occur as a result of employing staff, are a major part of most overhead cost budgets. It is not adequate simply to budget a lump sum for staff costs; there needs to be a detailed month-by-month analysis. Where additional staff are to be recruited during the budget year, each appointment should be specified in the following detail:

- job title
- salary and benefits
- date when employment will commence
- estimated capital expenditure required, such as company car, personal computer
- method and cost of recruitment.

It is unacceptably sloppy to budget for additional staff on the naive assumption that each person will join on the first day of the financial year.

When departmental overhead budgets are reviewed by higher-level management, the list of additional staff proposed should be challenged critically. The need to lay off staff when sales fall significantly below budgeted levels is costly, painful, time-consuming and generally demotivating, The most effective way to avoid the problem is to take a hard-nosed approach to any excessive or premature staff recruitment proposed in a departmental budget.

In the same way, all other overhead items should be budgeted accurately and supported by detailed working papers.

Large round sums for discretionary items such as trade exhibitions or press advertising should not be accepted. If a sum of, say, £150,000 is included in the budget, sufficient analysis must be provided, for example the exhibitions to be attended and the costs of each one. Press advertising should be broken down into the number of advertisements to be placed in each newspaper at an average cost per insertion.

Lump sums are equally unacceptable for items such as patent costs and overseas travel. The forecast cost for the current year, plus adjustments to reflect increased sales volumes and anticipated cost inflation, is unsatisfactory as a basis for budgeting costs such as these. Patent costs need to be budgeted in terms of the number of applications to be made in each country, multiplied by the average cost expected in each country. Overseas travel needs to be budgeted on an estimated basis, based on who will need to travel to which countries and for how long.

Capital expenditure

Once again detail is required; a lump-sum approach is unacceptable.

Individual projects should be listed, and the total capital expenditure costs estimated for each one. Associated revenue costs connected with a project should be estimated, so that these are not omitted from the appropriate overhead-cost budget; for example, the cost of additional software to be purchased with each personal computer. Equipment which needs to be replaced may be overlooked, such as the need for the existing telephone switchboard to be replaced by a larger one because the volume of calls can no longer be handled adequately.

The month in which each piece of capital expenditure will be invoiced by the supplier needs to be set out as part of the detailed budget. This may be thought excessive detail, but it is not. The combination of the proposed timing of capital expenditure and the differing working capital needs of the business during the year may exceed the company's borrowing facilities. The only way to avoid this is to plan the capital expenditure on a month-by-month basis.

Every manager needs to realise that the inclusion of a particular project in an approved capital expenditure budget does not automatically authorise the expenditure. Most companies rightly require a detailed commercial and financial justification to be presented and approved for all capital projects over a certain value. Equally, it may not make sense for a manager to be told during the budget year that a project will not be authorised because it was not itemised in the budget. If circumstances or priorities have changed, the manager should be allowed to carry out the proposed project provided that other capital expenditure items of a similar value are deleted.

The cash budget

For many types of business, cash is more difficult to budget accurately than profit. Even if actual sales are exactly in line with budget each month, there is no guarantee that customers will pay their invoices within the time allowed in the budget. Despite the inevitable inaccuracy, however, the cash budget is the most important budget of all. What is more, an annual cash budget is totally inadequate without additional detail. The cash budget must be calculated month by month, because there may be wide fluctuations during the year in the size of the overdraft required. Every item of cash must be included such as:

- cash received from customers based upon the budgeted period of time to be allowed for payment by customers

- interest payable or receivable

- payments to trade customers – based on a budgeted payment period from receipt of suppliers' invoices

- salaries and associated employment costs, such as pension and national insurance contributions

- capital expenditure, identified on a month-by-month basis.

Quarterly, six-monthly and annual outgoings need to be included, such as:

- rental and lease payments

- rates

- interim and final dividends

- advance corporation tax

- corporation tax

- insurance premiums

- bonus payments.

Monthly budget phasing

Obviously, to produce a monthly cash budget means that annual sales as well as operational costs and capital expenditure need to be budgeted on a month-by-month basis. This monthly analysis is often referred to as calendarising or phasing the budget.

Sales need to be calendarised on a monthly basis as accurately as possible. Most businesses have seasonal fluctuations in sales for a variety of reasons. These must be taken into account. Fortunately, history may provide a reliable guide for monthly budget phasing of sales. A useful exercise is to calculate the percentage of annual sales which took place in each month of the three previous years. The pattern may be sufficiently similar to provide a reliable guide for the budget year.

Equally, the budgeted annual profit must be phased monthly in order to determine whether or not the business is on course to achieve the budgeted profit quarter by quarter, but this does not provide a sufficiently early warning of a profit shortfall.

Effective monthly reporting

Monthly reporting needs to be prompt. Information which is sufficiently accurate, but includes some estimated figures, should be produced within two weeks of the end of each monthly or four-weekly accounting period. After all, in the following month any estimates which were made can be adjusted to the actual figures. Some companies take four or five weeks to produce monthly results, which is unacceptable.

Sales figures should be circulated daily, weekly and monthly because these give an indication of likely performance against the budgeted profit.

With the widespread use of computers, managers tend to be inundated with figures and printouts, but often lack sufficient useful information for management action. For example, a printout of all debtors requires time to be spent identifying those customers where further action is needed to collect outstanding debts. To compound the problem, some debtor printouts include all customers who have made a purchase during the financial year, even if they do not owe any money at present.

Summary information which is particularly useful for management action includes:

- a list of customers with a debt outstanding for either 60 or 90 days, perhaps listed in decreasing order of size to focus immediately on the largest amounts
- a list of any customers who have been allowed to exceed their authorised credit limit.

Computer-produced graphics, such as bar charts, pie charts and graphs, are a useful way of displaying a lot of data effectively. Sadly, not enough accountants who are responsible for producing monthly reports in companies make sufficient use of the facility. If necessary, a manager should request the accountant to present information using graphics.

A set of monthly reports needs to be accompanied by a narrative which comments upon and explains significant items. Without this the value of the figures is much reduced. When the monthly reports are to be reviewed at a board or management committee meeting, it is important that the reports and narrative are circulated in sufficient time for participants to have studied them before the meeting. Otherwise, not only is time likely to be wasted at the meeting but the discussion may also be unduly superficial.

Monthly reporting should not be restricted to financial statements produced by the finance department. The information presented should be what is needed for the effective management of the business, and may include the value or number of:

- proposals or tenders submitted
- orders received
- employee numbers compared with budget
- sales lost through unavailability of stock.

Financial year forecasts

Once a budget has been authorised, any revision should be firmly resisted, even if the cause was either unforeseen or beyond the control of the business, for example, an unexpected supplementary Budget from the government which increases the National Insurance contributions payable by employers. Managers will always be keen to seek a revision which reduces the budgeted profit, but a request for an increase is unheard of. As soon as a budgeted profit is reduced, this immediately becomes an acceptable standard of performance. The original budget is quickly forgotten.

This must not be allowed to happen. For a stockmarket-listed company to explain a disappointing profit performance in terms of some subsidiaries failing to achieve the budget would be unthinkable. It would be nothing less than an unacceptable and naive excuse. The management team must focus on the action to be taken to achieve the budgeted profit despite unforeseen setbacks.

Situations may arise where during the early months of the year, the actual profit is in line with budget but events have already occurred which will adversely affect the remainder of the year. Examples include a reduction in the level of enquiries or orders received, an adverse change in currency exchange rates and bank interest levels, or an unexpected increase in raw material costs.

Forecasts of profit and cash flow for the full financial year should be updated regularly to quantify the shortfall expected. The year-end forecasts should be updated at least quarterly. Better still, the forecast should be reviewed monthly and amended whenever necessary. Although the forecast will be prepared by the finance staff, it should be based upon discussions with the management team responsible for achieving it. Also, when a revised forecast is produced, it should be accompanied by a concise explanation of the changes and the reasons for them. The existence of a year-end forecast enables the board or management committee meeting to concentrate on what further action is to be taken to improve the forecast profit, rather than merely to review the result for the previous month.

Cash management

A receiver or liquidator is appointed when creditors are not paid sufficiently promptly. At the time, the business may have made a small profit in the current month, or the owners may feel confident that losses will be turned into profits during the next few months. The business may be expanding. All of this counts for nothing if creditors cannot be paid sufficiently quickly. Indeed, one of the causes of the problem may be that the business has been expanding too rapidly in relation to the amount of finance available.

However, it would be wrong to give the impression that cash management is needed only when a business might be facing receivership. Effective cash management is so important that every business should practise it 365 days a year, and to emphasise the point, 366 days each leap year.

Cash management is essential to optimise profit. Otherwise the amount of bank interest payable will be unnecessarily large. The finance staff do not manage the business, and neither do they manage cash. In both cases, they merely assist their colleagues in the management team. Cash management is a key executive task.

The foundation for effective cash management is a detailed cash flow budget, calendarised month by month, as described earlier. The other essential ingredients of cash management include:

- ensuring that customers pay promptly

- planning and controlling the amount of money tied up in stock and work-in-progress

- paying creditors sufficiently quickly to avoid either commercial disadvantage or financial penalty

- making sure that the level of overhead costs is affordable

- ensuring that adequate finance and bank overdraft facilities are available

- regularly monitoring performance against the cash flow budget

- maintaining a dialogue with the bank.

In addition, a prudent and rigorous approach is needed for capital expenditure decisions.

Debtor management

Debtor management is the process of obtaining prompt payment from customers. Some people imagine that all it involves is sending out invoices and writing reminder letters to customers who do not pay sufficiently quickly.

If only it was that simple, but nothing could be further from reality. Some of the main elements of debtor management are as follows:

Deposit with order

Whenever a custom-made product or service is supplied, a policy requiring a minimum deposit with the order should be adopted, unless there are valid reasons that this would damage the business. That none of your competitors has a similar policy is not necessarily a valid argument. Many companies and professional partnerships have found a surprising willingness among customers to make an initial payment, especially when the amount of work involved is explained to them.

Interim invoicing

Many services businesses overlook valid opportunities for interim invoicing which should be agreed at the outset as a matter of routine. The aim should be to invoice the client as soon as each stage is completed.

Prompt invoicing

When goods are supplied to a customer, the use of a multi-part stationery automatically produces the invoice at the same time as the items are despatched. Substantial delay may occur, however, before a service is invoiced.

Creditworthiness

Invoicing promptly is important, but it assumes that the customer has the ability and intention to pay. Problems may arise when supplying some private companies and individuals.

The credit status of private companies should be checked. Simply to request references from two other suppliers may be inadequate. The customer may pay these two accounts promptly purely to have references available. Equally, a bank reference may not reveal sufficient information about the customer. Also, beware of the customer placing two or three small orders and paying them promptly, only to follow these with a large order without the ability or intention to pay. An up-to-date credit-status report on a company can be purchased for a few pounds. Obviously, credit-status checks should be used selectively, rather than as a matter of routine, as some businesses do. The message is clear, however – if in any doubt, obtain a credit-status report.

It is difficult to check the creditworthiness of an individual. Outward appearances may create the impression of wealth but be nothing more than deliberate deceit. Cash with order should be requested or at least a worthwhile initial payment. A definite limit should be set for the maximum amount of credit to be allowed, and this should be strictly adhered to.

Credit limits

For many businesses, it makes sense to set a credit limit for each corporate customer, to establish the maximum credit to be allowed at any time. Whenever the limit would be exceeded by supplying another order received, the appropriate manager should be alerted. One phone call requesting payment of some of the existing debt before the next order is completed may produce a cheque immediately.

Eliminating excuses

Some customers have a habit of waiting until they are pressed for payment to point out the omission of basic information on the invoice, such as:

- customer order number
- supplier's VAT number
- delivery address.

They will point out that until this information is provided, the invoice cannot even be accepted. Once again, the remedy is simple. Ensure that all the relevant order information, including the terms of payment, is clearly and accurately stated on the invoice.

Prompt-payment discount

In theory, a discount on the invoiced price which ensures prompt payment seems like a good idea. The reality may be quite different. Two issues need to be considered: the cost and the benefit.

Some companies offer a 2.5 per cent discount for payment within seven days or ten days of the date of the invoice. If as a result a customer pays the invoice two months earlier than they would have without the incentive, then this is equivalent to an annualised cost of 15 per cent to the supplier. This is because a 2.5 per cent cost for receiving payment two months earlier must be multiplied by six to arrive at the annualised cost. When compared with the alternative cost of having a correspondingly large overdraft, this may appear reasonable in certain circumstances. If as a result of a 2.5 per cent prompt-payment discount, however, the customer pays only a month earlier, then the annualised cost to the supplier is 30 per cent, which is expensive.

Worse still, some large customers may pay their invoices after, say, a month and still automatically deduct the prompt-payment discount. Faced with this situation, some sales managers accept it rather than risk upsetting an important customer. This is far removed from effective cash management.

Requesting payment

On the day that payment becomes due, a request for payment should be made. A standard letter, produced by computer on flimsy paper with poor print quality and addressed simply to the accounts department is almost certain to have no effect. It is likely to be regarded as junk mail and consigned immediately to the wastepaper bin.

When an order is accepted, the name, position and address of the person who will authorise payment should be established. In a multinational company, invoices may need to be sent to a regional or head office located in another country. The request for payment should be addressed to the correct individual. It should ask that any reason why payment has not been made should be notified immediately. Telex or facsimile should be used rather than overseas airmail letters.

Telephone follow-up

If payment has not been received seven days from the first request for payment, a telephone call should be made to the person responsible for authorising payment. If the response is unsatisfactory, the person who placed the order should be telephoned and asked to obtain payment without further delay. If any queries are raised or reasons or excuses are given to justify non-payment, these must be answered or dealt with immediately. Sometimes two or three weeks will be taken to answer a query, which is effectively granting extended credit to the customer as a result of administrative incompetence.

Further action

If payment is not forthcoming, further action should be taken within a matter of days. Delay or, more accurately, procrastination is likely to reduce significantly the chances of receiving payment at all. According to the amount and country concerned, either a debt-collecting agency or a solicitor should be instructed.

Stock and work-in-progress management

The cost of holding raw materials, production work-in-progress and finished goods ready for sale is alarmingly high. Various studies carried out by major companies have demonstrated that the annual cost of holding stock is between 25 and 40 per cent of the value of stock. In other words, every £1m of inventory costs between £250,000 and £400,000 a year to hold in stock.

At first sight, these figures seem difficult to believe. When the various elements of cost are identified, however, the reality becomes apparent. The cost of holding stock and work-in-progress includes:

- interest charges on the finance required

- occupancy costs such as rent, rates and any service charges for the premises
- heating and lighting of the premises
- insurance costs
- damage and theft of stock
- storage equipment and mechanical handling costs.

Effective inventory management requires continuous communication between marketing, sales, production and purchasing staff. In some companies, detailed production and purchasing budgets will be produced. One thing is certain, however: either the actual volume or the mix of sales is likely to prove significantly different from the budget. This means that:

- marketing staff should alert the other departments to forthcoming promotional campaigns and the forecast impact on sales
- sales staff should continuously notify both production and purchasing staff of changes in the volume of enquiries and orders received, so that schedules may be amended accordingly.

Every effort should be made to reduce the time taken in the production cycle to turn raw materials into finished goods for sale. The concept of just-in-time inventory management should be adapted by small businesses to get tangible results for themselves. These techniques are not the sole preserve of large companies.

Creditor payment

To delay paying creditors until legal action is commenced may be costly and counterproductive. For example, if tax is not paid by the due date, the Inland Revenue will charge interest and this is not an allowable charge against taxable profits. Some suppliers will seize any opportunity to increase the price quoted in order to compensate themselves for anticipated slow payment. When a delivery or service is required urgently, the request for help from a slow-paying customer may be met with little enthusiasm.

The ingredients for effective supplier management and creditor payment include ensuring that:

- no order is placed without an agreed price. This happens surprisingly often, especially on urgent orders, and is an invitation to the supplier to choose the price to be paid
- each order is properly authorised

Figure 11.01 Cash-flow forecast (six-month example)

	Jan		Feb		Mar		Apr		May		Jun		Total	
	Projected	Actual	Projected	Actual	Projected	Actual	Projected	Actual	Projected	Actual	Projected	Actual	Projected	Actual
Receipts														
Sales – cash														
Sales – debtors														
Loans														
Other receipts														
A Total receipts														
Payments														
Cash purchases														
To creditors														
Wages and salaries (net)														
PAYE/NIC														
Capital terms														
Rent/rates														
Services														
HP/leasing arrangements														
Bank/finance charges														
Loan repayments														
Other payments														
VAT (net)														
Corporation tax, etc.														
Dividend														
B Total payments														
Opening bank balance														
Add to B if overdrawn														
Subtract from B if credit														
C Total														
D Closing bank balance (difference between A and C)														

- payment is properly authorised. The order may have been supplied, but payment needs to be authorised to confirm that the quality and performance are satisfactory

- early payment is made to benefit from attractive discounts. The benefit to be gained by taking advantage of the prompt-payment discount may be substantially more than the cost of additional overdraft interest

- quantity discounts are taken for placing large orders, with the flexibility of changing call-off rates to suit varying demand. Some suppliers offer substantial percentage discounts for large orders. The negotiation of flexible call-off rates avoids the risk of excessive stocks if the demand is lower than expected

- the budgeted creditor-payment period is adhered to on an overall basis. If the budgeted credit payment is, say, 60 days, then this will be achieved by a selective approach to the speed with which each creditor is paid.

Overhead costs

A common cause of a cash flow crisis is the creation of substantial overhead costs in anticipation of future sales, which do not occur as quickly as expected. For example, the development of a major new product may be substantially more costly than expected and take considerably longer to achieve. Or the level of sales achieved from additional branches may be much lower than expected. It is not enough simply to produce a cash flow budget based on optimistic sales projections. It is essential to be satisfied that sufficient finance will be available if actual sales should be considerably lower than expected.

Another trap to be avoided is when the budget is based on an ambitious and continuously increasing sales pattern throughout the year. The staff required to achieve the budgeted sales growth need to be recruited and trained to make it happen. Caution is needed with recruitment elsewhere in the business, however, because if the sales growth is less than expected, the overhead burden will be a drain on both profit and cash flow.

Adequate finance

Cash flow is difficult to predict accurately. It depends not just on the volume and timing of sales during the year, but on the speed with which customers pay their invoices as well.

Safety first must be the motto. It is dangerous, not merely unwise, to assume that the finance required is simply that indicated by translating an ambitious sales budget into a cash flow requirement. If the actual sales fall below budget, there is likely to be a disproportionate effect on profit and cash flow. This applies particularly to services companies with overhead costs which are largely fixed in the short term over a wide range of sales levels, such as insurance brokers or estate agents.

The cash flow consequences of a lower level of sales must be quantified, and the board must be satisfied that adequate finance is available. The sources of external finance available include:

- issuing more 'paper' such as ordinary shares, preference shares, convertible loan stock, loan stock and loan notes
- sale and leaseback of freehold properties
- leasing and hire purchase of assets
- fixed-term loans
- debt factoring
- bank overdrafts.

Monitoring cash now

It is not acceptable simply to check the bank statement each month to be satisfied that the balance is in line with the comparable figure in the cash flow budget. The situation may be much worse than budget because:

- some major payments, such as VAT or property rents, were paid but not cleared for payment in time to appear on the month-end bank statement
- the finance staff have been slowing down payments to suppliers in order to keep within the cash flow budget or overdraft limit
- a large unscheduled payment needs to be made next month.

The effective monitoring of cash flow requires each month:

- the actual receipts and payments to be compared with budget to identify differences which would otherwise remain hidden for a time
- the cash flow forecast to be updated for each of the next three months and the remainder of the financial year in total to identify the need for corrective action.

In some large companies, the cash flow forecast for the next month is prepared on a week-by-week basis for tight cash control.

Bank contact

Some companies mistakenly adopt the policy of avoiding contact with the bank manager wherever possible. This is shortsighted. Sooner or later, the time will come when the support of the bank is needed to help the business handle a temporary cash flow crisis. When this happens, the goodwill created by regular communication with the bank is helpful.

The minimum communication required is to telephone the bank if the overdraft limit is to be exceeded, even if only for a day. It is a basic courtesy and gives the bank confidence that the business knows what is happening to the overdraft. If the overdraft limit is likely to become inadequate, a meeting should be arranged to explain the circumstances and to present an updated monthly cash flow forecast.

Other companies go further than this. The bank will be supplied with a copy of the audited accounts and the annual phased cash flow budget and management accounts at intervals during the year. This is not essential. It does, however, give more confidence to the bank. It is possible, too, that the bank manager may be able to offer an alternative approach to meet the financing needs which is more attractive than an increased overdraft.

An example of the layout of a cash flow forecast is given earlier.

Profit management

Every manager must understand the anatomy of profit, but, perhaps surprisingly the statutory or conventional profit and loss account is not sufficiently revealing. The profit and loss account needs to be broken down into variable and fixed costs, to show the marginal profit, for effective profit management.

Variable costs

Variable costs are those costs which increase or decrease directly in proportion to changes in sales volume. Examples of variable costs are:

- the materials used to make a product
- royalties payable on each sale
- carriage cost when using a parcels carrier rather than a company delivery fleet.

The proportion of variable costs in relation to sales varies widely according to the type of business. The variable costs of a discount retailer, the actual product costs, will be a large percentage of sales. For a ten-pin-bowling alley, the percentage of variable costs will be low. It would be wrong to assume, however, that a low proportion of variable costs will automatically create high profits and vice versa. The profit will be affected by the level of fixed costs within the business, regardless of the level of sales achieved.

Fixed costs

Fixed costs remain unchanged in the short term despite changes in sales volume, unless specific action is taken. These costs tend to be related to time rather than volume, such as monthly salaries and depreciation. Examples of fixed costs are:

- rent

- rates

- depreciation

- salaries

- cleaning costs.

Clearly, some costs are partly variable. An obvious example is the cost of the telephone. There is a fixed charge and a variable charge. An important issue for a manufacturing company is the classification of production labour costs. These are directly connected with the cost of the product, but not necessarily variable. Few companies recruit and lay off production staff directly in relation to sales volume. The likelihood is that the labour force is regarded as a fixed resource in the short term, and modest changes in sales volume are absorbed by changes in inventory levels.

For the sake of easy calculation, some companies identify the costs which are truly variable and classify the remainder as fixed. This is not entirely accurate, but is probably sufficient for the purpose.

Marginal profit

Marginal profit is defined as the sales revenue minus the variable cost of sales. An important figure to know for profit management is the percentage marginal profit:

$$\text{Percentage of marginal profit} = \frac{\text{Sales revenue} - \text{variable cost of sales} \times 100}{\text{Sales revenue}}$$

If the sales of a company are £10.0m and the variable cost of sales is £5.5m, then the percentage marginal profit is:

$$\text{Percentage of marginal profit}$$
$$= \frac{£10m - £5.5m}{£10m}$$

$$= \frac{£4.5m = 45\%}{£10m}$$

It must not be assumed that a high percentage marginal profit will ensure high profits. An extreme example illustrates what may happen. Some years ago an electronics company formed a subsidiary company to make and sell silicon chips. It was realised at the outset that the minimum viable size of production unit and the essential number of technical staff required would lead to substantial losses in the early years. During the third financial year, a 74 per cent marginal profit was achieved. However, because actual sales were still much lower than the available capacity, the fixed costs were 205 per cent of sales revenue. So a loss of 131 per cent of sales resulted. In sharp contrast, the next year produced sales nearly three times higher and a modest profit was achieved.

Some managers assume that percentage marginal profit achieved by each product or service group will be virtually identical. In many businesses, the reality is dramatically different. For example, if the overall average marginal profit is 45 per cent, the figures for individual product or service groups may range from 30 to 60 per cent or even more.

Effective profit management requires maximising not just the total sales value produced from a given level of fixed costs, but also the total amount of marginal profit which can be generated.

Unless the percentage of marginal profit is known for each product or service group, profit management is reduced to shooting in the dark. What is worse, customers have an uncanny knack of recognising bargain prices, even if the supplier is unaware that a bargain price is being offered, which means a best-selling product or service may result from the sales price reflecting a lower-than-average percentage marginal profit.

Ignorance of marginal profit percentages can be disastrous. A computer component manufacturer suffered a fall in selling prices from $2.25 to $0.79 in less than 18 months, because of overcapacity among suppliers. A once profitable company rapidly suffered heavy losses. A policy decision was taken to capture more market share to eliminate the losses, but unfortunately they increased further. A company doctor was called in to save the business. It was rapidly established that the variable cost was $0.89, 10 cents higher than the selling price, and that there was little scope for improvement using the existing facilities. The company had been leapfrogged by competitors using the latest technology to reduce costs substantially.

A knowledge of the percentage marginal profit produced by each product or service group enables the manager to increase profit by:

- ensuring that the marketing effort is biased towards the products and services producing above-average percentage marginal profit

- directing sales resources towards the above-average percentage marginal profit lines. If appropriate, differential sales commission incentives should be introduced

- value engineering below-average products and services to increase the percentage marginal profit by reducing the variable cost where possible; and also incorporating features which will command a disproportionately higher sales price

- making sure that any new products and services introduced will at least maintain the overall average marginal profit achieved by the business.

Other ingredients of effective profit management are:

- a knowledge of the break-even point of the business

- the management of product profitability

- the profitability achieved from key customers

- the dangers of marginal pricing.

Each of these aspects will now be described.

Break-even point

The break-even point of a business is the level of sales at which neither a profit nor a loss results.

A knowledge of the total fixed costs and the overall percentage marginal profit allows the break-even point to be calculated:

$$\text{Break-even point} = \frac{\text{Fixed costs}}{\text{Percentage marginal profit}}$$

The higher the percentage marginal profit, the greater is the impact of a change in sales volume on the profit before tax, and vice versa.

Product and service profitability

In many businesses, the calculation of the profit or loss before tax achieved by a product or service group involves guesswork. The reason is that many of the staff and facilities in a complex business are shared by more than one product or service group. This means that accountants apportion or allocate a fair share of the common costs to individual products or services. Words such as 'apportion' and 'allocate' give a feel of scientific accuracy when a degree of informed guesswork is what is really involved. As a result, the profit or loss before tax calculated for a product or service group may be significantly inaccurate. This can lead to decisions to discontinue sales of a product on the basis of allocated as well as specific costs. If there is then nowhere else for the allocated costs to go, the overall profit will be reduced.

Customer profitability

Customer concentration is growing. Many businesses have one or more customers each of which account for at least 5 per cent of total invoiced sales. Often these customers are more demanding than smaller ones. In addition to receiving lower prices or being given quantity discounts, other costs may be incurred as well.

When a customer accounts for more than 5 per cent of total sales, the percentage marginal profit for the customer should be calculated. If any additional overhead costs are incurred for a particular customer, these should be identified as well.

Marginal pricing dangers

This section has concentrated upon the importance of marginal profit analysis to optimise customer, product and service profitability. Marginal pricing, in contrast, may well undermine existing profitability instead of improving it.

If there is spare capacity in a business, regardless of whether it is a manufacturer or a services company, it could be argued that marginal pricing should be adopted. In other words, the surplus capacity should be sold at cut prices as long as some marginal profit is gained from each sale.

Arithmetically this appears attractive, but the real dangers are:

- the cut-price work undermines the normal priced business, or even substitutes for some of it

- a price war with competitors may be sparked off and prices generally may be reduced.

If it does make sense to utilise spare capacity by accepting business with lower profitability, important aspects are to:

- limit the amount of cut-price business and the period during which it will be offered, otherwise it may be so attractive to customers that overall profitability will fall

- offer a more basic specification than normal, to justify and preserve the price differential

- direct the cut-price business towards a different type of customer or country, so that the base business is not undermined.

Financial analysis for decision-making

Few major business decisions are so clear-cut that financial analysis can be safely ignored, because the benefits are so overwhelming. Some managers delegate all the financial analysis to an accountant. As the financial analysis could make or break the decision to proceed, this is an abdication of responsibility rather than delegation of the calculation involved.

Equally, many managers are unfamiliar with the most effective techniques of financial analysis to assist decision-making. Words such as discounted payback periods, internal rates of return, net present values and sensitivity analysis seem proof enough that financial analysis for decision-making is beyond their grasp. Such an assumption is entirely wrong.

Financial analysis for decision-making requires:

- a knowledge of which technique is appropriate
- forecast of future revenues, costs and cash flows
- an understanding of the answer produced by the computer or calculator.

Technique

There is wide acceptance that the appropriate financial analysis technique for decision-making is based upon cash flow and not profit. Decisions should be based upon:

- future cash flows
- incremental and differential cash flows
- company-wide cash flows.

Each of these terms is sufficiently important to require further explanation.

Only *future cash flows* should be taken into account when making a decision. Past and irretrievable cash flows should be ignored.

The amount spent to date, and the extent to which costs have exceeded budget, are irrelevant for decision-making purposes. Regardless of whether the project proceeds or not, development costs to date will have to be charged to the profit and loss account. The decision needs to be based upon whether or not a further outlay is justified by the cash flow benefits to be gained from the current estimate of future sales.

Incremental and differential cash flow is simpler than it sounds. Cash flows which will continue whether or not the decision to proceed is made should be ignored and only the differences taken into account.

Costs which exist already and will not increase should be ignored completely and no attempt should be made to apportion a share of these costs when doing the financial analysis for decision-making.

The *company-wide* impact on cash flow must be assessed, not merely the effect upon the department initiating the project. It would be wrong, for example, for a division developing a new product to ignore the cash flow implications for, say, the warehousing and distribution division. Either a new warehouse or an extension to the existing one may be needed, involving a substantial cash outlay. This must be included in the project evaluation.

In a similar way, the requirement of additional working capital must not be overlooked. Often working capital is a significant part of the overall cash flow investment in an expansion project.

Evaluation

The criteria most commonly used to evaluate the cash flow projection for a proposed project are:

- pay-back period
- discounted pay-back period
- percentage internal rate of return
- net present value.

Pay-back period

This method simply calculates the time required for the incremental cash outflow to be recouped. For example, consider the following:

Initial cash outlay:	£40,000
Annual cash inflow:	
Year 1	£5,000
2	£10,000
3	£15,000
4	£20,000
5	£10,000

The pay-back period is 3.5 years, as it will be halfway through the fourth year before the cumulative cash inflow equals the initial cash outflow of £40,000.

There are two obvious shortcomings of using the pay-back period for decision-making:

- interest costs on the cash outflow are ignored
- no consideration is given to either the duration or amount of cash inflow after the pay-back period.

Discounted pay-back period

The discounted pay-back method in discounted cash flow (DCF) analysis takes into account the interest costs on the cash outflow. So the discounted pay-back period is the time required to recoup the initial cash outflow, at an assumed rate of interest. No consideration of what happens afterwards is taken into account.

Some companies assume a standard rate of interest when using discounted pay-back periods, on the assumption that the current interest rate may be temporarily high or low and not typical of the likely average interest rate during the pay-back period. Also, by choosing a standard rate of interest, a maximum pay-back period can be set so that a decision to proceed can be taken. In the previous example, the pay-back period was 3.5 years. If a standard interest rate of 10 per cent is assumed, the discounted pay-back period would be 4.3 years. Using a typical bank overdraft rate of, say, 15 per cent, the discounted pay-back period would be in excess of 5 years.

Percentage internal rate of return (IRR)

This is often referred to as the percentage IRR (or as the DCF rate of return). If the cash flows from a project are calculated to give a 17 per cent IRR, after tax, this means that the weighted average return, taking into account the changes in the net cash outflow which are expected to occur during the project and calculated net of corporation tax, over the assumed effective life of the project, is 17 per cent.

This allows a company to set a minimum percentage IRR for projects to be authorised. Many companies require a minimum percentage IRR of at least 15 per cent net of tax.

The effective life of the project is not necessarily the useful physical life of the assets. For example, some purpose-built electronic test equipment may perform satisfactorily for at least 20 years. The effective life of the project may be only five years, however, because by then the market demand for the particular product will have expired.

Net present value (NPV)

Net present value is another variation of discounted cash flow techniques, but the most abstract one for managers to use. Generally, the percentage IRR is much more widely used and easier to understand.

As some companies do use net present value, often abbreviated to NPV, it will be described briefly. The NPV is the estimated value of all the future cash outflows and inflows, discounted at a standard percentage rate chosen by the company. For example, the NPV of the cash flows in the previous example, discounted at 15 per cent, is net outflow of £1,280.

This seems to beg the question: is this an acceptable return or not? One method of answering this is to calculate a NPV Index, defined as:

$$\text{NPV index} = \frac{\text{NPV, at assumed rate of return}}{\text{Maximum cash outflow}}$$

This still requires a second calculation, compared with the percentage IRR method.

Sensitivity analysis

Sensitivity analysis allows the impact of different possible outcomes to be evaluated easily. It is sometimes described as 'what if?' analysis, because it answers the question 'what if such and such were to happen?'

Typical outcomes which can be evaluated are:

- What if development work costs 5 per cent more than forecast?
- What if the sales launch is delayed by six months?
- What if sales in the first year are 10 per cent below forecast?
- What if sales prices are 1 per cent higher or lower than forecast?

The management role

The manager responsible for the project or investment must play a major part in the forecast of sales volumes, selling prices and operating costs from which the cash flows will be calculated. An accountant may well be better equipped than the manager to produce the cash flow analysis, but the accountant must not be allowed to make assumptions about sales volumes, selling prices, staffing levels and operating costs. This is the area in which the manager must provide the requisite knowledge of the marketplace and the method of operation.

Similarly, the manager should be better equipped than an accountant to understand the main vulnerabilities of the project. So the manager should suggest that specific 'what if?' calculations are carried out. The accountant should carry out additional 'what if' calculations to highlight other situations in which the rate of return would be particularly sensitive.

Equally, the manager must understand not only what the answer calculated by the accountant means but also why the company requires a given maximum rate of return. Simply to achieve a rate of return comparable with current overdraft interest rates is totally unacceptable, for several reasons:

- Managers tend to be optimistic when projecting the future cash flow to be achieved from an investment, so allowance has to be made in the rate of return required.

- Occasionally, a project will fail substantially or be aborted after considerable expense has been incurred.

- In some businesses, about one-fifth of total investment does not generate a cash flow, because it is required for essential replacement, refurbishment or to meet legislation.

- Last but not least, there should be some return achieved for the benefit of shareholders to reward them for the commercial risk involved.

So it is not surprising that many companies require a rate of return of at least 25 per cent a year, before the effect of corporation tax is taken into account.

Investment risks and rewards

Many companies set one required rate of return for all investments regardless of the differing risks and uncertainties involved. This has the merit of simplicity. It could result, however, in decisions to:

- reject projects such as an investment to reduce existing costs, where there is a minimum of risk and uncertainty, because the return falls short of the required minimum

- approve speculative projects, such as an investment to launch a new product in an overseas market.

Merchant bankers and financial institutions recognise the need for an acceptable balance between potential risk and reward. Different rates of return are required for investment in management buy-outs compared with venture-capital finance for newly formed companies.

A small proportion of large companies adopt a similar approach by setting different rates of return according to the degree of risk involved in various categories of projects. Possible categories are:

- improved efficiency in the existing business, such as investment in automation, mechanical handling, improved test facilities

- expansion of existing products or services in existing markets and countries

- diversification into a new product or service in an existing market or country, or vice versa

- a new product or service in a new market or country.

Clearly, the rate of return required should increase in each of the above categories. To set differential rates of return requires considerable expertise. Nonetheless, there is a case for adopting a flexible approach, even if somewhat subjectively, to investment decision-making. Low-risk projects perhaps should be approved even if the required return is not quite enough. In contrast, an investment which involves considerable diversification and only just achieves the necessary return requires the utmost scrutiny.

Application

The cash flow analysis techniques described in this chapter are widely applicable. They can be used to evaluate:

- *Lease versus buy decisions.* The cost of outright purchase and regular lease payments can be compared to calculate the percentage IRR (internal rate of return), which is the effective percentage annual cost of leasing.

- *Make versus buy decisions.* The differential cash flows of making in-house compared with buying the product or service are used to calculate the percentage IRR.

- *Expansion projects.* The cash outflow required to finance capital expenditure and working capital is compared with the incremental cash inflow produced throughout the assumed project life to calculate the percentage IRR.

- *Company acquisitions.* The cost of acquisition is compared with the total incremental cash flow benefit to the acquirer to calculate a percentage IRR.

Commercial factors

It must never be forgotten that an acceptable rate-of-return calculation is not sufficient to justify an investment decision. In addition, the proposed investment needs to be:

- consistent with the chosen corporate strategy and commercial rationale of the business

- the most suitable method to achieve the required goal, after consideration of the different alternatives available

- an acceptable balance between potential reward and interest risk

- acceptable to customers, suppliers and staff, where appropriate.

12 Human resources management

Although this chapter is entitled 'human resources management', a clear distinction will be drawn between issues relating to the strategic management of people and the role performed by the human resources function. It is a common error in this field for people to confuse what these two aspects of people management comprise within organisations. How an organisation chooses to manage its people is very different to what the human resources function does on a day-to-day basis.

The context for strategic people management

'People are our most important asset' is a time-honoured organisational cliché and no chief executive or senior manager would disagree with the essential truth of the statement. Yet the reality for many organisations is that people continue to remain a much undervalued, undertrained and under-utilised resource. However, the signs are that this rather dated perspective and approach is at last changing. In recent times there has been a new business and organisational focus on people management as a major source of competitive advantage.

Accelerating technological change and increased global economic, regulatory, social and demographic change demand organisations that are fast moving and responsive. Commercial challenges and financial/economic pressures mean that all businesses must now absorb and manage change at a faster rate than ever before. Companies continue to restructure, downsize, develop alliances, de-merge and acquire new businesses at breakneck speed. This means that the people who work in organisations are increasingly viewed as central to developing new levels of flexibility in response to this complex business environment.

The huge explosion and boom in the telecommunications and technology world from the late 1990s did much to promote a new emphasis on people management and although this has cooled of late, there are indications that it has had a lasting impact on the way in which we think about people management and business performance. The dotcom boom pushed the issue of people management to the top of the business agenda and led to many new trends and innovations in people management.

The move from an industrial to knowledge-based era

Some of the changes that have been taking place in the global economy have been described as a fundamental shift from an industrial to a knowledge-based era. In this context, knowledge is seen as the real originator of wealth and value in competitive terms. This has given rise to concepts such as the management of knowledge and intellectual capital. We have moved from a world of fixed assets, where value was attached to physical items such as plant and equipment, to a world of flexible assets and perspectives. In such a world ideas and imagination represent a major source of competitive advantage, and the owners of this type of capital are of course individuals. This can be seen in many global companies which increasingly manage a 'brand'. In effect, they outsource all activities that require some form of manufacture to other low-cost organisations. They then concentrate on developing the 'brand' and extending it into new and even more profitable concepts or streams of activity. This approach relies increasingly on vision, imagination and innovation to succeed and continually revitalise and refresh the brand. Increasingly, 'making things' is seen as a tough business to be in as there are too many companies in the world who can do it better and cheaper.

The people capital of an organisation can be divided into three distinct areas:

1   **People capital** consists of the skills, knowledge, attitudes and imagination of individuals employed. This knowledge is, of course, highly mobile as people can leave an organisation. As was once said, Microsoft is a company whose assets go home every night.

Figure 12.1 **Forms of human capital**

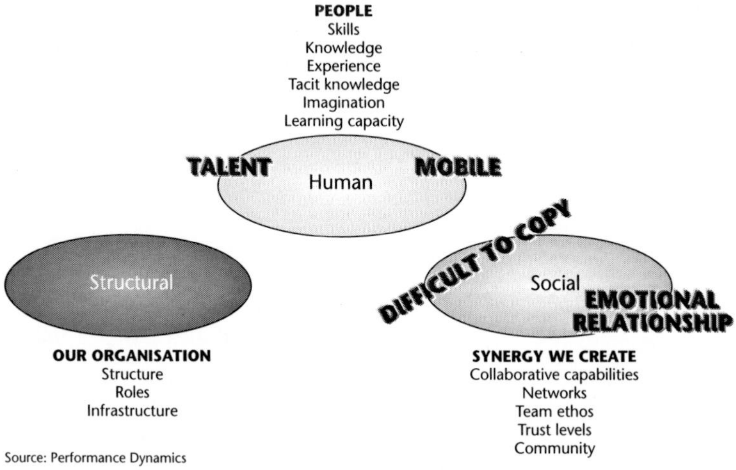

PEOPLE
Skills
Knowledge
Experience
Tacit knowledge
Imagination
Learning capacity

TALENT   MOBILE
Human

DIFFICULT TO COPY

Structural

Social   EMOTIONAL
RELATIONSHIP

OUR ORGANISATION
Structure
Roles
Infrastructure

SYNERGY WE CREATE
Collaborative capabilities
Networks
Team ethos
Trust levels
Community

Source: Performance Dynamics

2   **Structural capital** is defined as the roles and organisational structure that make up how the business is organised.

3   **Social capital** is perhaps the area of most significance in the search for competitive advantage as it is the most difficult to copy. It can be described as the synergies that are created by combining all the assets of the organisation together. It is the ethos and culture of the organisation.

An excellent example of a high level of social capital and to a lesser extent structural capital has been Dell computers. Michael Dell's business model has been the subject of countless books and studies. Yet other competitors seemed unable to compete with his success. It could be argued that Dell managed to create a form of social capital that is extremely difficult to copy, despite the fact that there has been no secret about the business model. Some competitors have been able to mimic his organisation or structural capital but still found it difficult to compete. Dell established a unique competitive position.

People and business performance linkages

A recent survey of chief executives revealed that two of the most significant problems in trying to implement a new business strategy were:

1   not having people capable of delivering the strategy

2   a failure to train people effectively to implement and execute the strategy.

As access to the latest manufacturing processes, financial software controls and information technology becomes ever more widely available, one of the few areas left that offers real sustainable competitive advantage for organisations is their people capability. While information technology continues to provide enormous competitive advantages, the need to manage the people and technology interface becomes even more critical. Senior managers might consider how much existing IT capability is unrealised in their organisation because people have not been properly trained to exploit it. At the same time, for example, as email might be said to have profoundly changed business and personal communication, it might even be said to be making some organisations grind to a halt as people fail to use the technology correctly. By not training people to utilise and harness the enormous benefits of email you can run the risk of creating a more inefficient organisation.

Nevertheless, technology continues to redefine our organisations. Customer service functions are being reorganised to take account of intelligent machine and systems diagnostics, which reduce the need for expensive service engineers. Many faults can now be repaired online. Call centres are managed from different parts of the world and it matters less and less where the work is carried out. But we should pause and reflect on some aspects of the advances in technology. Is it always the case that new advancements result in improved benefits to the customer? There is some evidence to suggest that organisations are not getting the balance right.

Whatever happened to the customer?

Throughout the 1980s and early 1990s most corporate employees were bombarded by seminars, articles, books and internal initiatives extolling the virtues of customer service. Now it seems Customer Relationship Management or CRM became the big buzz word, at least within the IT world. Companies invest heavily in trying to mine their customer data and identify ever more segments. The idea is that everything customers get is tailored to their needs. But today you have to ask yourself: whatever happened to all those good intentions about the customer and service? It seems in some businesses as though customers no longer matter – they have been sacrificed in the face of relentless cost pressures and the need to show a quick return. Peter Drucker, a well-known business guru, once said that 'the purpose of a business is to create a customer'. Two critical questions that all businesses need to be asking themselves in today's tough business environment, particularly given the impact of the internet, are:

- What new customers are we creating?

- How easy are we to do business with?

British Airways (now part of IAG) used to have an excellent telephone booking system for business users. It was free, fast and efficient and you spoke instantly to a real person. Today you are encouraged to book via the website that seems to carry a big corporate mentality and ethos. BA has again saved some costs but no doubt alienanted loyal customers who no longer feel they are getting value for money or good service. BA's apparent vulnerability to strike action hasn't helped its cause.

It also seems that other businesses, in their rush to use new technology and in particular the internet, have lost focus. Some businesses seem intent on using the internet in order to avoid having to deal with customers. For example, a recently purchased digital organiser quickly fails to work. Obtaining a telephone number or contact address to sort out the problem with the company proves almost impossible. You have to navigate their website to progress your complaint. After finding a web page that seems remotely related to your specific query, you are asked to enter numerous details and then wait for an email response which takes about a day. Despite repeated requests for a telephone number or a quick call back, you are told it has to be done via the web. Welcome to the customer-focused digital era.

John Cassidy in his book *dot.con* commented, 'the internet is great as a research tool, a mail service and a vehicle for sexual fantasy, but it is not going to rewrite the rules of business or turn stupid business ideas into gold'. Unfortunately he has not quite been proved right on either count but what return does the customer get for doing all the work? The answer all too often is a firewall of voice-recorded messages that drives ordinary customers to despair. Some businesses differentiate their brand and service by offering real people at the end of their telephone lines but more and more do not.

Nothing will stop the development of new technologies, but in some businesses there is an urgent need to recognise the human dimension in delivering customer value. In this context, people management is being taken more seriously within many organisations. You cannot deliver world-class quality or service if you have poor people management. Some business leaders have recognised this fact.

The search and race for talent

Talent attracts talent

There is little doubt that technology is creating a technocratic elite – people who are highly trained, mobile, scarce and much sought after. Software engineers, social networking experts, programmers and web/app designers are all examples of highly prized knowledge workers.

In the late 1990s the powerful McKinsey consultancy produced a report titled *The War for Talent*. It was a major milestone in the people and business performance world as it moved the whole issue of talent management up the corporate agenda. The fact that the world's most influential strategic consultancy had taken on the subject meant it became a major focus within the business world. Suddenly all CEOs were examining their approach to talent management.

One way of viewing this new level of interest is to see the employee contract with a company as an interaction between the organisation's attractiveness and its ability to attract different levels of talent. Figure 12.2 shows that in today's digital world there are three key elements involved in the contract:

- **The economic** – I'll stay here or join because they pay quite well.

- **The social** – I'll stay here or join because I like the people; they are like me and I enjoy working with them.

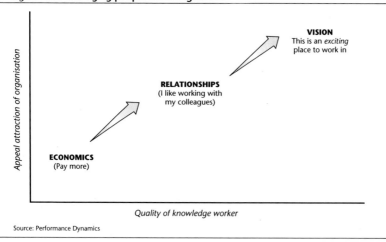

Figure 12.2 **Managing people in the digital era**

Appeal attraction of organisation (y-axis)

VISION
This is an *exciting* place to work in

RELATIONSHIPS
(I like working with my colleagues)

ECONOMICS
(Pay more)

Quality of knowledge worker

Source: Performance Dynamics

- **The vision** – I'll stay here or join as this is an exciting place to be; I can learn and grow.

In today's environment it is frequently the vision issue that enables the best companies to employ the best talent. Apple, Google and Microsoft all benefit immensely in their ability to attract and retain talent because they are seen as exciting places to work. Such companies have become magnets for talent. A critical element in developing magnetism is to create a place of work and cultural environment where people feel that they can excel. This then needs to be backed up by superior people-management processes.

This search for highly prized 'gold-collared' knowledge workers is an increasing challenge for global organisations. All businesses are trying to ensure that they get their fair quota of talented staff. This has increased pressure for more innovative pay and reward schemes as well as a more sophisticated approach to career development. When this book was first published in 1991, we were witnessing the shift from cash to equities as the major incentive to high performers. Indeed, the late 1990s was characterised by a huge rush to equities as the means of motivating the best talent. This was a time when for a small elite there seemed to be little interest in cash – stock options were the real magnet for talent. Many software and technology companies, such as Microsoft and Cisco, were literally creating groups of millionaires among their staff. This prompted discussions about how you keep a young 28-year-old independently wealthy employee motivated. Of course, with the more recent correction of the capital and equity markets, there has been a swing back to cash incentives as a means of motivating talented staff. At the time

Microsoft announced that it would be offering more cash incentives to its staff. Figure 12.3 sets out some key organisational elements that attract talent.

Figure 12.3 **What drives employees?**

- Quality of the company
- Culture of the organisation
- Image of the organisation
- Quality of their bosses
- Personal empowerment
- Personal development
- Benefits and rewards

Source: Performance Dynamics

Despite the fluctuation from equities back to cash and the general peaks and troughs of economic cycles, people management is becoming a more central strategic issue. No longer can global organisations rely simply upon pay as the main weapon in recruitment. Knowledge workers demand more. Organisations need to offer a total development package of which pay is just an element. Training and development opportunities are major items on a knowledge worker's shopping list. Indeed, the opportunity to grow and develop in a company is increasingly seen as a key differentiator when it comes to attracting the brightest and best. This has prompted some companies to think about becoming an 'Employer of Choice', where the status of their brand in the marketplace encourages talented people to seek them out. Such an approach demands that an organisation is able to offer world-class people-management processes and programmes.

The rise of the social agenda and the question of work-life balance

Changing social values and environmental concerns are also having an impact on people's attitudes towards the world of work, their employer and career planning.

Research is emerging which indicates that the aspirations and values of managers are changing. Stanford Research International (SRI) in the US has identified a new breed of manager who seeks a career that mirrors his or her own personal values rather than those of the organisation. The London Business School has conducted research into middle-management values and aspirations, and has identified serious dissatisfaction with existing organisational life and the pressures on middle managers. Its conclusions pose major questions for future career development and planning activities. Many managers, it appears, are becoming tired of being asked to do 'more with less'. The attraction of working for large businesses is losing its appeal. Many managers are seeking greater independence and autonomy away from the pressures and stress of corporate life.

Yet recent research presented by Peter Nolan of Leeds University on behalf of the Economic and Social Research Council in the UK concluded with some interesting observations. The study contrasted key trends in the UK working population from the 1990s to the 2000s. It revealed that contrary to popular thinking, job tenure in the UK had increased rather than fallen. Fifteen years ago the average job tenure was six years and two months. In 2004 the average length of job tenure was estimated to be seven years and four months. It was also calculated that nine out of ten employees were in permanent employment, and even more surprising was the fact that only 7 per cent of the UK workforce was self-employed. This last finding was lower than that recorded in the mid-1980s.

Just as the research showed that the UK did not seem to be turning into a nation of self-employed knowledge workers, it also went on to debunk the notion that technology was reinventing jobs. The study revealed that at that time, when it came to technology, 70 per cent of senior managers used the internet. This figure fell to 20 per cent for supervisors and technicians and 15 per cent for other workers. It concluded that the jobs where stability and growth had beckoned were in traditional services and retailing occupations and not the cutting edge of technology.

When it came to the issue of the work-life balance, the study did reinforce some conventional thinking. In the UK:

- one-third of men worked more than 50 hours a week

- the percentage of men who were satisfied or happy with their working hours had fallen from 35% to 20%

- the percentage of women who expressed satisfaction with their working hours had fallen from 54% to 26%.

The research concluded that a major issue in the world of work was how to achieve a work-life balance. Recent evidence suggests that this trend is likely to continue and will force organisations to revisit their people-management policies. Already the courts have intervened in cases where severe stress and illness appears to have been induced by an excessive work regime. Further studies showed that people were generally less happy than they were 20+ years ago. Technology, business improvements and wealth may have increased, but people are becoming more dissatisfied. The uncertainty and pressures of today's corporate world are creating lots of disaffection. Burn-out now seems possible among managers in their 30s rather than their 50s. This is an unhealthy trend that will need to be addressed by more innovative people-management approaches. Some corporations are already offering sabbaticals and more flexible methods of working as a means of holding on to highly talented and expensive people.

The ethical corporation and leader

At the same time, environmental issues and concerns are forcing organisations to reconsider their business methods and operations. In recent years, major corporations such as Shell, Nike and BP have fallen foul of a new sense of antagonism towards businesses that appear not to behave in a supposedly environmentally friendly or ethical manner. Shell came under attack for its decision to sink the Brent Spar oil platform in the Atlantic (a decision later vindicated) and for its activities in Nigeria. Meanwhile, Nike suffered considerable adverse publicity for engaging product suppliers in Asia who used child labour. The Nike sweatshop labour incident led to an exposure of other global players such as Wal Mart, Gap and Walt Disney, all of which have been forced to review their methods and processes for engaging suppliers in the developing world. Many sports products in the US now carry labels that indicate the absence of any child labour in their production. BP's Gulf of Mexico oil spill revealed much about its safety procedures and the company's brand suffered as a result of its handling of the crisis as well as the environmental problems it caused.

Actions and responses to such incidents are seen as part of a growing trend towards consumer and shareholder activism. The Shell Brent Spar incident resulted in a major boycott of petrol stations in Germany. BP's Gulf disaster resulted in changes in leadership, procedures and perception. Consumer incidents and protests in the US also show that corporations now have to take their brand image seriously when it comes to behaving in a fair and equitable way. This is no doubt having an impact on how future employees will feel about working for a major company.

There is much evidence to suggest that we still have a long way to go when it comes to ethical behaviour. The collapses of Enron, Andersen, WorldCom,

Ahold, Lehman Brothers and Madoff Investment Securities indicate something of a loss of moral compass in some corporations.

The Enron debacle and scandal clearly raised the issue of corporate leadership. But Enron is not the only high-profile company to be challenged by the role and behaviour of its leaders. Past leaders of Sotheby's in the US have been jailed and heavily fined for serious offences relating to illegal price fixing. The leaders of mighty organisations such as Merrill Lynch and Rank Xerox faced major US Securities and Exchange Commission investigations into their business affairs and received heavy fines. The once hero of European business, Percy Barnevik of ABB, was forced to make a public apology and to return some £37m of pension arrangement which did not meet with satisfactory measures of shareholder governance. Sir Brian Moffat of Corus received a salary increase of 100%, while his strategy resulted in 6,000 steel workers being sacked; the strategy failed and Corus went on to face yet more crises. Perhaps most amazing of all David Duncan, the Andersen partner responsible for Enron, turned star witness for the US government's prosecution. Andersen, one of the world's greatest corporate success stories, was destroyed in a matter of weeks.

In January 2002, Al Dunlap, former CEO of Sunbeam, was fined $15m for falsely reporting performance. Incidentally, his nickname was Chainsaw Al, based on his appetite for cost cutting. In April 2002, the New York State Attorney General charged Merrill Lynch analysts with privately referring to certain stocks as 'crap' and 'junk' while at the same time recommending them to investors. Barnevik's disputed £61m pension (see above) was reported in one Swedish newspaper as equivalent to what 7,967 nurses would earn in one year. In 1999, the pay of Sir Peter Bonfield, CEO of BT, rose by 130% to £2.53m – not bad for someone who destroyed shareholder value at an enormous rate. The most celebrated example of corporate greed has to be Lord Simpson and John Mayo of Marconi, who eroded a cash mountain of £2.6bn and delivered instead a £4.4bn debt and an almost worthless company. But they still argued for their £1m plus pay-offs as part of their contractual arrangements. Indeed, John Mayo subsequently tried to sue Marconi for outstanding monies. Legally they may be right, but from a meritocratic and moral perspective many might argue that they are bankrupt. Despite this debacle, Lord Simpson held on to several board positions in other companies for months afterwards. More recently the unseemly rewards of 'Bankers', despite their actions having contributed to a banking industry meltdown and economic hardship, have yet again cast the spotlight on corporate ethics.

The 1990s was a decade when celebrity CEOs were very much in vogue, but it would seem that this cult of leadership is now over. But what of the impact of such behaviour on the issue of people management? Already there has been widespread condemnation of so-called 'fat cat' leaders whose rewards have no relationship with their underlying business performance. In some cases, payment schemes appear to have been designed to reward failure, with chief executives receiving huge bonuses when there has been no shareholder value created.

It is to be hoped that in the next few years there will be a greater emphasis on ethical behaviour among business leaders. The Enron debacle led to a tougher system of regulation being imposed on corporations, whilst controls to inhibit reckless banking activities are being sought in the wake of the recent financial crisis; no doubt worried shareholders, governments and regulatory authorities will continue to seek more protection. This will affect many aspects of how people in organisations are expected to operate. There is little doubt that the corporate world had a tough start to the new millennium. Capital investors have been shocked, but more importantly have lost money as a result of some corporate excesses that have been driven by inappropriate leadership behaviour. There is likely to be more restraint and control in the coming years and a far greater emphasis on ethical behaviour both at both an individual and corporate level. This will filter through to all aspects of how a corporation does business.

Figure 12.4 **The HR business model**

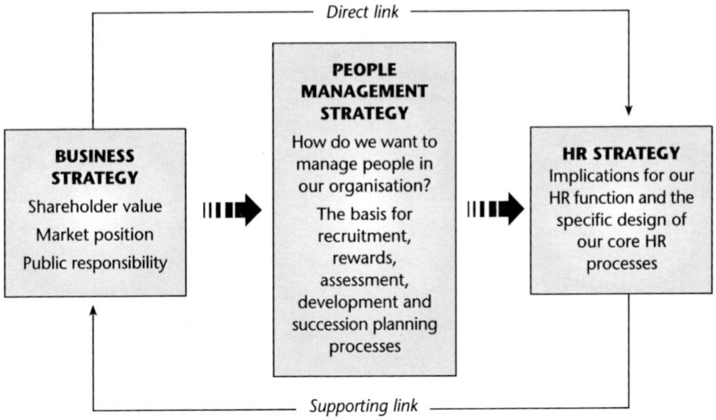

Source: Performance Dynamics

Developing a human resources (HR) strategy

Faced with the challenges of global complexity and uncertainty, how can an organisation develop a more focused and coherent approach to managing people? Just as a business requires a marketing or information technology strategy, it also requires a human resources (HR) or people strategy. Some commentators have argued that an HR strategy is a contradiction in terms and that it has to be integrated with the overall business strategy. The latter is certainly true, but in developing a HR strategy three critical areas (see Figure 12.4) have to be addressed so as not to fall into the trap of developing something that is isolated from the key business issues:

1   **The business strategy** – What kinds of people do we need to attract and manage to run our business to meet our strategic business objectives?

2   **The people management strategy** – How do we want to fundamentally manage people within the business?

3   **The HR strategy** – What are the implications of the above two areas for how we organise and manage our HR function? – What kinds of people management programmes and initiatives must be designed and implemented to attract, develop and retain staff to compete effectively?

It is important to review these three areas sequentially, but at the same time the process of developing the complete strategy is an iterative process that requires constant refinement. The starting point has to be defining the fundamental strategic business goals and objectives (Step 1). In order to consider the people dimensions, it is necessary to know what the business is trying to achieve in terms of markets, customers and return on investment. Without a strategic business context, any HR strategy will prove useless.

When examining the people and HR dimensions of the strategy, managers too often confuse what the HR function does (Step 3) with what the business leaders need to decide in relation to managing their people within a business (Step 2). In Figure 12.4, the business leaders must first define the overall architecture for people management and then pass this to the HR function for the development of detailed HR processes and programmes in the areas of recruitment, development, rewards and communications, and so on.

How a leadership team wants to manage people at a strategic level may require them to consider in detail how they recruit, reward and develop people. Figure 12.5 illustrates some continuums that can help to focus the debate. It is important to stress is that there is no right or wrong involved in this discussion and analysis. It is for the business leaders to decide if they want a high-performance type of organisation where non-performance is viewed negatively or a more developmental type of culture. Similarly, it is for the business leaders to decide if they want to develop talent from within – with the intention that senior posts will be filled by an internal market of available talent – or whether they are happy to recruit externally as and when needed. It is these high-level decisions that can help shape the over-arching HR policy and strategy. Too often this type of debate fails to take place and the HR function is left to struggle on without a clearly aligned top-team view or perspective on people management. As a consequence, the HR function is stereotypically criticised for being disconnected from the business and delivering processes that are not relevant.

Figure 12.5 **Managing people at a strategic level**

How do we want to manage people at a strategic level? **What kind of organisation do we want?**	
HIGH PERFORMANCE	**DEVELOPMENTAL**
Up or out career track	Long-term career track
Primarily performance-oriented appraisal	Primarily developmental appraisal process
Reward linked to individual performance	Pay linked to team performance
High variable pay as a percentage of compensation	Low variable pay as a percentage of compensation
High performance related turnover	Lower performance related turnover
Aggressive external resourcing of roles at all levels	Minimum external resourcing of roles at middle and senior levels

Source: Performance Dynamics

HR managers might facilitate and be part of this discussion, but it is the business leaders who should ultimately decide. The outcome of this type of discussion is that the HR managers will then have a high-level architecture to begin shaping the details of their various processes and programmes in the areas of rewards and development.

Figure 12.6 **Assessing current and future organisation capability**

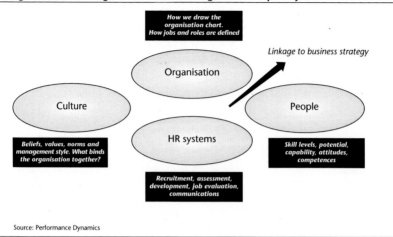

Source: Performance Dynamics

To help assess the current and future organisation they require, senior managers will need to focus on four dimensions of an organisation's performance (see Figure 12.6).

1   Culture – the beliefs, values, norms and management style of the organisation.

2   Organisation – the structure, job roles and reporting lines of the organisation.

3   People – the skill levels, staff potential and management capability.

4   HR – the people-focused mechanisms which deliver the strategy, such as communications, training, rewards, career development.

In managing the people element of their business, senior managers frequently focus on only one or two dimensions and neglect to deal with the others. Typically, companies reorganise their structures to free managers from bureaucracy and encourage more entrepreneurial flair but then fail to adjust their training or reward systems. When the desired entrepreneurial behaviour does not emerge, managers often seem confused at the apparent failure of the changes to deliver results. The fact is that seldom can you focus on only one area. What is required is a strategic perspective aimed at identifying the relationship between all four dimensions.

If you require an organisation which really values quality and service, you not only have to retrain staff, you must also review the organisation, reward, and appraisal and communications systems. The pay and reward system is a classic

Figure 12.7 **Developing a human resources strategy: explicit link between business and human resources strategy**

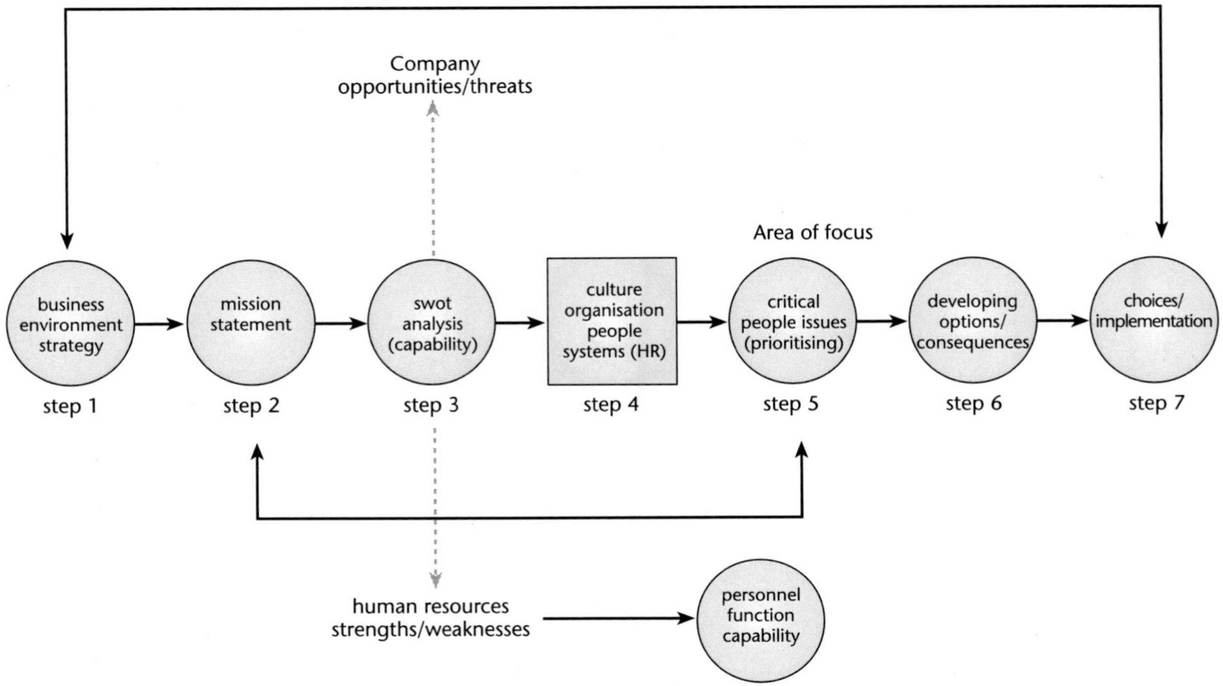

problem. Frequently, organisations have payment systems which are designed around the volume of output produced. If you then seek to develop a company which emphasises the product's quality, you must change the pay systems. Otherwise you have a contradiction between what the chief executive is saying about quality and what your payment system is encouraging staff to do.

Outlined below is a simple but highly focused process for helping to build a HR strategy. It uses some simple and well known strategic models to help build a current and future assessment of people capability. The power of the process is in shaping the right questions and issues for discussion and providing a source of focus to shape future people-management programmes and initiatives in line with the broader business strategy.

There are seven steps to developing an HR strategy and the active involvement of senior line managers should be sought throughout the process (see Figure 12.7). This ensures that there is an even balance between the functional HR experts and the line perspectives which is so important to producing a credible outcome. Of course if you take an iterative approach, the process outlined below should be fully incorporated into the wider business planning process. It could be that in some cases a business strategy is fundamentally flawed by the absence of some core people elements. For example: 'On reflection we just do not have the people capability to be able to deliver that kind of business growth or profit ambition!'

Step 1

- Define, clarify and understand your business strategy. Utilise strategic documents and scrutinise them for people capability and competence issues.

- Highlight the key driving forces of your business – for example, technology, distribution, cost, product innovation, speed to market.

- What future challenges face the business? Growth, increasing cost pressures, competitor activity – what role do people play in shaping responses to these challenges?

- What are the implications of these driving forces for the people side of the business?

- What new skills and capabilities will be required to deliver the future strategy?

- What is the fundamental people contribution to bottom-line business performance? If product or service innovation is critical, then how do we promote and develop that capability among our people?

- If technology is critical, how well do we manage technology in the business? What processes are in place to build our people capabilities in this area?

Step 2

- Develop a Mission Statement or Statement of Intent relating to the people side of the business. Articulate how you want to engage people in the business and what you want people to value.

- Consider incorporating this 'people component' into a broader strategic statement as many companies do.

- Do not be put off by negative reactions to the words or references to idealistic statements – it is the actual process of thinking through the issues in a formal and explicit manner that is important. Keep asking what core people skills and capabilities contribute to business success. But at the same time beware 'glib' statements.

Step 3

- Conduct a simple but exhaustive capability assessment of the organisation. Consider using the classic SWOT (strengths, weaknesses, opportunities and threats) analysis of the organisation. It is a simple but powerful process. However, make sure that you challenge and test some of the assumptions you are making when formulating the SWOT analysis. For example, are you really that good at pricing or distribution?

- Focus on the internal strengths and weaknesses of the people side of the business. Consider the current skill and capability issues. Think about the following skills and core capabilities:
  - project management
  - IT and MIS
  - finance
  - marketing
  - sales
  - R&D
  - production
  - distribution
  - managing alliances and joint ventures
  - licensing
  - legal.

- Vigorously research the external business and market environment. Highlight the opportunities and threats relating to the people side of the business. What impact will/might they have on business performance? Consider skill shortages and the impact of new technology on staffing levels.

- Then conduct a separate capability assessment of your HR or personnel department. Complete a further SWOT analysis of the department – consider in detail the department's current areas of operation, the service levels and competences of your HR staff.

- What areas do they excel in?
    - Union relationships
    - People development
    - Recruitment
    - Innovative reward strategies
    - Line relationships and general business credibility
    - Service provision – payroll and admin

Step 4

- Having conducted a broad assessment of both the people side of the business and your HR function, you then need to conduct a further detailed analysis that concentrates on the four key areas of COPS:
    - Culture
    - Organisation
    - People
    - Systems

- Setting your analysis firmly against your broader business strategy, consider where you are now in relation to each of the four dimensions and then decide where you want to be.

- This process can be challenging as it may force you to confront difficult choices. For example, is your business really customer focused? What it might mean to try to move from being product focused to being customer focused? Or from a sales-driven to a marketing-driven culture? Such discussions are not easy as they challenge the essence of an organisation's past and future.

- Are you satisfied that your current organisation structure and job roles support your business strategy? Or are you facing the need to fundamentally redesign your organisation so that it will support rather than hinder the future strategy? A detailed COPS analysis begins to identify issues for discussion and clarification.

- What gaps exists between the reality of where you are now and where you want to be?

- Exhaust your analysis of the four dimensions.

Step 5

- Once you have completed Step 4, go back to your business strategy and examine it against your SWOT and COPS analyses. You are now trying to test the viability of the strategic objectives against your organisation's people capability.

- Having reviewed your detailed SWOT and COPS analyses against the business strategy, identify the critical people issues – the issues that you must address in order to be sure of delivering your business strategy.

- Prioritise these critical people issues.

- Consider what will happen if you fail to take action and address these issues. Remember you are trying to identify areas where you should be focusing your efforts and resources.

Step 6

- For each critical issue highlight the options available for managerial action – generate, elaborate and create – don't go for the obvious choice. This is an important step because frequently people go for the known rather than challenging existing assumptions about the way things have been done in the past. Think about the consequences of taking various courses of action.

- Consider the mix of HR systems needed to address the issues:
  - Do you need to improve communications, training in key areas or your rewards strategies?
  - Are all your HR processes correctly aligned? Do they support and reinforce each other? Or do some work against each other?

- What are the implications of these needs for the business and the HR function?
  - Is the HR function correctly organised to deliver these future requirements?
  - Will certain priorities need to change among line managers?

- Once you have worked through the process it should be possible to translate the action plan into a broader set of objectives. These in turn will need to be broken down into precise targets for the specialist functional areas of HR:
  - performance management
  - executive development
  - organisation design and development
  - rewards
  - recruitment and sourcing
  - competence development
  - communication.
- Develop clear action plans for the critical issues you have identified. Remember strategy is all about focus and making choices. Finally agree targets and dates for the accomplishment of the key targets deliverables.

Step 7

- Monitor implementation and evaluate achievement of action plans.

Figure 12.8 **HR function: core process**

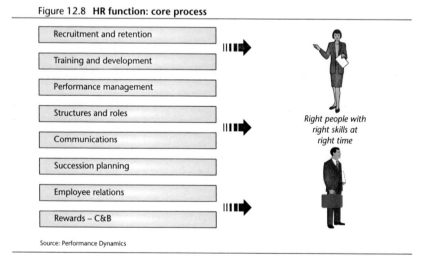

Source: Performance Dynamics

The ultimate purpose of developing a human resource strategy is to ensure that the objectives set are mutually supportive of the wider business plans. It should also ensure that all the core HR processes are aligned, so that, for example, the reward and payment systems are integrated with training and career development plans. There is little value or benefit in training people only to frustrate them through a failure to provide ample career and development opportunities. What is required is a clearly aligned set of HR processes so that the organisation ultimately gets the right people with the right skills at the right time (see Figure 12.8).

Managing change

Whether it is a change in business direction, a major restructuring or a merger or acquisition, managers have to be able to manage change. Indeed, it might be argued that in today's world to manage change is to manage the status quo. Change is everywhere and we have to try to embrace it rather than fear it. Yet as individuals we all crave a sense of stability and continuity. One of the issues relating to the work-life balance dilemma stems from the fact that in today's corporate world too many people are so fearful of losing their job that they believe they have to keep up with all the changes and work without question or complaint. The result is enormous pressure and stress, and people who do not embrace change are likely to become victims in today's organisation. Yet it seems we can still learn a lot about how to manage change more effectively.

When it comes to change scenarios, the reactions of staff are often underestimated and as a result badly handled. Managers often seem better prepared or trained to deal with the 'what' than the 'how' of change. The result is often badly implemented change plans that overrun and fail to deliver the expected results.

There are five major issues to consider when managing complex organisational change:

1   The difficulty of trying to identify all the problems likely to arise during the change process.

2   Estimating correctly the amount of time needed to communicate and 'sell in' the change.

3   The lack of commitment to the change – the change is frequently desired by 'them' not 'us'.

4   The impact of new crises emerging during the change process – this often results in a change in direction, and the loss of critical mass and further support for the original change.

5   The time it will take to implement the change.

Why do people resist change?

It should be emphasised that not all changes are resisted. It has been said that people do not oppose change, only that they oppose being changed. The inclination of people to oppose change is often offset by the possible rewards associated with any change or the prospect of them gaining from any new and positive experiences. Salary increases are generally welcomed, but where organisational change involves disruption to established relationships or the status quo more negative reactions are likely to occur. Indeed, where changes are threatened it is frequently the manner in which a change is proposed or sold that provokes the resistance. Often the change process is distorted by ineffective or poor communications. Yet the fact is that change does often generate a sense of fear and this is frequently underestimated or overlooked by managers who may be pushing the change agenda. On a personal level, the questions posed by change are very real and they need to be addressed when managing the process:

- Why do we need to change?
- Will I keep my existing role or job?
- What will my new role and responsibilities be?
- Will I get a new boss?
- Will they change the structure or role of my team, unit or department?
- Will they change my title or status?
- What about the future plans for my team, unit or department?
- Will this damage my future career prospects?
- Will I have to move home?
- Can I trust the new management?
- What is in it for me – rewards, responsibilities, scope and workload?
- When will the changes happen?
- What are the options open to me if I accept or reject the changes?

During periods of large-scale change such as a merger or acquisition, these types of questions, when left unanswered, can create havoc with business performance, as people focus their energies internally rather than on the customer. It should also be remembered that these questions are frequently asked by senior managers who themselves are being asked to implement the change. Little wonder that the process of managing organisational change can prove so difficult.

Of course once an organisation has started to introduce major change, managers must manage other factors that impose even greater pressures on the organisation (see Figure 12.9). The majority of these issues demand considerable planning, and even then it is not always possible to convince people of the need for change.

Figure 12.9   **Managing major change – some common issues**

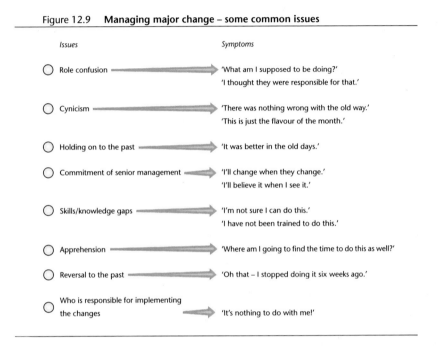

Issues	Symptoms
Role confusion	'What am I supposed to be doing?' 'I thought they were responsible for that.'
Cynicism	'There was nothing wrong with the old way.' 'This is just the flavour of the month.'
Holding on to the past	'It was better in the old days.'
Commitment of senior management	'I'll change when they change.' 'I'll believe it when I see it.'
Skills/knowledge gaps	'I'm not sure I can do this.' 'I have not been trained to do this.'
Apprehension	'Where am I going to find the time to do this as well?'
Reversal to the past	'Oh that – I stopped doing it six weeks ago.'
Who is responsible for implementing the changes	'It's nothing to do with me!'

The question of corporate culture

It is now quite common to hear chief executives talk of the need to change the culture of an organisation in order to manage change and improve performance. Yet despite this level of interest corporate culture still remains, for many managers, undefined. But culture does play a significant role in any process of change. Perhaps the most useful definition of corporate culture is 'the way we do things around here'. Corporate culture reflects the management style, ethos and values of an organisation and has a number of core dimensions:

1   Beliefs and values

What fundamentally binds the organisation and people together. What is truly valued and appreciated across the organisation. For example:

- I believe this organisation stands for quality

- I think this organisation is striving to be a world leader in software design
- Engineering excellence
- Product innovation
- Ethical standards
- Public service

2 Norms

The behaviours that are deemed acceptable within the organisation. For example:

- Respect for authority and hierarchy
- Approaches to problem solving
- The manner in which meetings are run
- Use of first names, dress standards
- The standards of performance required

3 Style

This encompasses the general tone of the management style and day-to-day behaviours within an organisation. For example:

- Open-door approach
- Autocratic or paternalistic people management
- Deference to authority
- Collegiate or individual-based approaches towards decision-making
- The manner in which rewards and punishment are used
- Use of information – open versus 'need to know basis'

Another way of viewing these cultural dimensions is to think of beliefs and values as existing below the surface of the organisation and the norms and style as being above the surface. It may be difficult to assess what people are thinking in the case of their beliefs and values. However, it is relatively easy to identify an organisation's management style. Observing how managers manage and the extent to which standards of performance, quality and customer care are applied say a lot about the culture of an organisation. Consider, for example, how an organisation tackles certain business problems. Does it appoint a committee or assign an individual with responsibility for solving the problem? The way meetings are run is another visible example of an organisation's culture. Do meetings start and run to time or do they start late and drift? Are the meetings run with an open and positive atmosphere or are they closed and secretive? Consider how managers behave towards each other. Do they work together in a mutually supportive manner or is their behaviour characterised by a lot of politics and infighting? These types of observations provide clear indications of an organisation's culture.

Figure 12.10 **Culture as accelerator/brake**

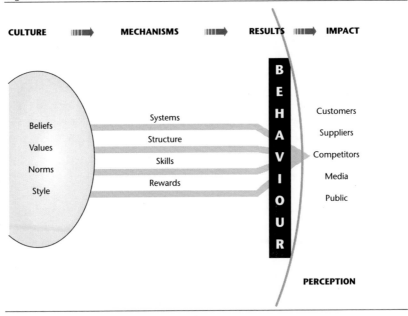

The crucial point is that culture can be both an accelerator and a brake on an organisation's performance. But it is also frequently difficult to manage – culture is there but it is much more difficult to manipulate than a balance sheet. Culture is often in the heads of the management of a business. It involves the shared mental models and assumptions that managers have about their business, competitors and markets. To help illustrate this point the model developed by Colin Price, formerly of Price Waterhouse and then with McKinsey Management Consultants, is helpful (see Figure 12.10).

Ultimately, an organisation is judged by its performance in the marketplace. In this context, the perception of a business or organisation is critical to its success. The image of an organisation is predominantly shaped by the behaviour of staff towards its suppliers, customers, competitors and the other key stake-holders, including the media and government. On one level, it is the way in which a receptionist answers the telephone or greets visitors. On another, it is the manner in which a salesman deals with customers, and whether invoices are paid on time and quality goods are delivered to time and cost. All these interactions with the outside world help to shape perception.

Perception is shaped by behaviour and that ultimately determines profitability. What are the ways in which managers try to shape people's behaviour? Traditionally, organisations have influenced people by using various levers:

Systems

A change in systems is one of the most favoured ways of trying to influence people's behaviour. Huge investments in information technology and software are associated with trying to reduce costs and improve efficiency. It is expected that by providing managers with up-to-date management information they will be able to make faster and more effective business decisions and hence improve business performance and ultimately profitability. SAP is a prime example of a piece of software that tries to shape how an organisation does business.

Organisation structure

Managers spend a lot of time trying to develop the most appropriate organisation structure to manage their business. Arguments over centralisation, decentralisation, divisionalisation and matrix structures are common in every organisation. Indeed, some managers would argue that there have been clear indications of which structure is in vogue at a particular time. Managers also redesign job roles and responsibilities. The intention of changing an organisation structure or job roles is to effect a change in people's behaviour, by either exerting more control over staff or giving greater autonomy and freedom to managers.

Skills training

Any form of skills training involves an active attempt to change behaviour. Customer care, quality, management, financial and technical skills training aims to encourage people to operate and perform in a different way at the end of the training programme or intervention.

Rewards

Changes in pay and reward systems are also ultimately aimed at redirecting staff behaviour. Pay is a classic management lever – 'if you want to get a change in behaviour then hit the pocket' is the accepted mantra. Huge amounts of time and effort go into developing new payment schemes and incentive programmes. In the case of production workers, it is to improve quality or output. In the sales function, changes to commission and incentive schemes are directed at improving sales of a particular product range. It may be aimed at encouraging the sale of some new after-sales service contracts or some other value-added service. The end objective is the same: 'we want you to do something differently and we will reward you for doing so'.

Although these change levers often work effectively, there are many occasions when large amounts of money and management time have failed to deliver the required changes in behaviour and subsequent business performance. These failures can often be attributed to management's failure to pay enough attention to the impact of the organisation's culture. Some people argue that in today's world we should not pay for change as it encourages a negative and costly reaction the next time a change is required. Instead we should simply promote the notion that change is the accepted norm and that we have to embrace it as an everyday occurrence.

Customer care and quality campaigns – a warning from the 1980s

In the 1980s there was enormous interest in customer service and care. Inspired by the success of airlines such as SAS and British Airways, organisations involved in all sectors from manufacturing through to financial services have endeavoured to emulate them. In many instances managers invested heavily only to be disappointed with the results. All too often senior managers failed to recognise the huge amount of management attention and commitment required to successfully drive a customer-care initiative. Many campaigns became little more than 'smile campaigns', in which front-line staff were encouraged to smile politely to customers and wear new uniforms. Little work was done to address more fundamental issues relating to the product's quality or internal management systems because there was a failure to understand the need to change the culture of the business.

BA's 'Putting People First' campaign illustrated the depth and complexity of the company's approach. Integrating actions encompassed BA's culture, organisation, people and systems, and included:

- a shake-out of senior management
- the introduction of performance management structures
- huge investment in training
- wide-ranging customer-care initiatives
- large-scale reorganisation
- the real commitment of senior management.

The last point is perhaps the most important of all. Little culture change occurs in any organisation unless senior managers show commitment to it and, more importantly, are prepared to force it through. The fact that Colin Marshall, as chief executive of BA, attended the majority of staff seminars on customer care became part of BA's success legend at that time. His actions and highly visible support left the organisation in no doubt that the management was serious about the initiative and that a commitment to quality had to become a fundamental belief.

Today of course BA faces far bigger threats from the low-cost airlines that are dramatically eating into its markets by offering a radical alternative. It has also been tested by not only one of the worst airline recessions in history but also by global terrorism. This highlights another important business lesson. You can have the right business model for a time, but you have to be able to refresh it as new competitors come along and attack your markets. Another crucial element in understanding culture is that it also has to be renewed. In the case of BA, many customers might say that it lost the focus on the customer that it had in the 1980s, becoming arrogant and aloof. This again is the challenge of corporate culture. If your business is very successful, you may soon start to think that you know best and are invincible. This can be very dangerous as you may lose sight of the customer.

How to change your corporate culture

Managers often ask if there such a thing as a good or bad culture. The fact is that there is no right or wrong culture. Every organisation has a culture whether management thinks consciously about it or not. The real question is whether the culture matches the strategy of the organisation.

Corporate culture must be constantly tuned to the business strategy and environment.

The risks of having a strong culture are as follows:

- *Obsolescence* – the culture becomes outdated, the marketplace moves or a new competitor enters, resulting in a mismatch between your strategy and culture. A good example of this is Marks & Spencer, whose culture ultimately led it to an enormous crisis in the late 1990s. It was so successful that it came to believe it was invincible and that it knew best. As a result it failed to detect new competitors such as Gap and Next emerging in the retail sector. It soon began to look slow and jaded and started to lose customers. Marks & Spencer became too inward looking and arrogant and as a result experienced a major crisis and subsequent transformation which restored some of its strength. More recently internet retailing has wrong-footed traditional bricks and mortar retailers.

- *Resistance* – the culture inhibits change and thus the introduction of new ideas and approaches; core values and beliefs can be extremely difficult to change.

Changing an organisation's culture is not an easy task. Although many people put forward 'quick fix' solutions, most managers who have been involved in culture change agree that it takes years rather than months to effect a lasting change. Indeed, it can be argued that cultural change is a continuous process which managers must never let up on. Marks & Spencer's transformation took three to four painful years. Jack Welch at GE took many years to achieve the transformation from a moribund industrial monolith to a dynamic world leader in financial services and leading technologies.

There is strong evidence that corporate culture was a major factor in the case of the dramatic collapse of both Enron and Andersen as well as the more recent banking crisis. Both Enron and Andersen succeeded in developing dynamic and powerful business cultures that ultimately became unhealthy and corrosive in certain ethical positions. It led some managers to believe that they would always be proved right so they did not need to worry about the consequences of their actions.

The prerequisites for success in managing cultural change are:

1   a clear sense of direction or vision as to what the new organisation wants to achieve

2   the clear commitment and ownership of senior management regarding the change

3   the ability to manage people's expectations. Not everything changes overnight and managers and staff need to be prepared for setbacks

4   an effective communications programme which emphasises the role of middle managers and staff in the change process and secures their commitment to and ownership of the changes

5   the commitment of resources to drive the change and train staff for the new.

It is also important to remember that in any change process people focus more on how their managers behave than on what they say. Developing elaborate statements relating to an organisation's mission or sense of purpose and direction can be helpful. But it is the actual delivery of the words that is the real test of the process. People soon detect any inconsistency between what is being said and how managers and leaders are behaving. Managing in a way that is consistent with what they are saying can be very painful for some managers. Ultimately, nothing changes unless behaviour changes.

How to manage change

- Cultivate an appetite for change. If change is seen as the norm it will be more acceptable.

- Develop trust. Much depends on the degree of confidence and trust that people have in a management team.

- Watch the timing. Take time in introducing change, create a favourable atmosphere and give people time to get accustomed to an idea before implementing it. The fast introduction of change without consultation rarely works.

- Provide information. Keep people informed about the change. Provide a full explanation for the change. Highlight the benefits of the change.

- Do not expect instant conversion. Engage in participative decision-making as a means of developing commitment. Often people will not simply stand up and support the change – they will need time. Simply talking at people provides information, but mutual decision-making results in far higher levels of acceptance and ownership.

- Provide clear and focused messages. Stick to the core reasons for the change and constantly repeat and reinforce them. Too many complex messages result in confusion.

- Avoid criticism of the past. Concentrate on positive aspects of the change, and avoid criticising any past actions if possible

- Ask questions that force people to think. Get people thinking about the logic for the change and then get them to think through the issues by posing lots of questions. For example: What happens if we do nothing? What are the alternatives open to us?

- Aim at an acceptable solution. Do you need to get everyone on board? Will 80 per cent of staff be enough to push things through? Be pragmatic and reasonable when thinking about outcomes.

- Listen sympathetically. Give people the opportunity to voice their concerns and issues. Make sure you really are listening and not just hearing the concerns. Where possible deal with the questions and concerns.

- Be wary of 'negative suggestions'. For example: 'It would be fine if we could do so and so, but it is not really possible in a firm like ours.' Such comments are frequently masking a form of resistance to the proposed change. Try to get to the real issues and probe behind the initial suggestion.

- Emphasise continued support and help both during and after the change.

- Once agreement seems certain, get the plans agreed quickly, including a programme and timetable.

- Give others a share of the credit. Make sure all parties are acknowledged for their contribution. Make it a team approach to change

- Provide retraining where applicable to help staff make the transition.

- Finally remember that being logically right can be psychologically wrong. Change involves emotions as well as logic. Make sure you do not underestimate the emotional or psychological factors. The fundamental challenge of most change is to develop an emotional rather than a logical commitment to the proposals.

How to plan the introduction of change – managing stakeholders

The model detailed below can be used to help map out the stakeholder issues that will have to be managed in any change process. It can be used by the project manager planning the change, or by a planning team or the people involved in the change process itself. The benefit of the model is not that it provides the right answers but rather that it provides a clear structure and framework for identifying and dealing with all the issues that might emerge from the various key stakeholders.

Mapping the key players involved in the change – the wheel technique (see Figure 12.11)

1   List the *outcomes* you wish to achieve by introducing the change. What are the objectives involved with this change process?

   - The more specific your objectives and outcomes are the easier it will be to begin developing solutions.

   - An example might be: 'To improve the output of a work group from 70 to 90 per cent of what is theoretically possible'.

2   List the objectives and outcomes (in an abbreviated form) in the centre of a flip-chart.

3   Draw out from the centre a number of 'spokes' to form a wheel (there is no limit to the number of 'spokes' needed to form the wheel).

4   Write the names of key individuals or groups affected by the change in the various 'spokes':

   - These are people who will be affected either directly or indirectly by the proposed changes.

- Also include the key stakeholders or people who can influence the change by providing their support or opposition to the proposed change.

- There are no special rules about whether a person should be placed in a 'spoke' on their own, or put in with a group. Simply reflect on whether the individual has any power to either assist or impede the change.

Figure 12.11 **Illustration of the wheel technique**

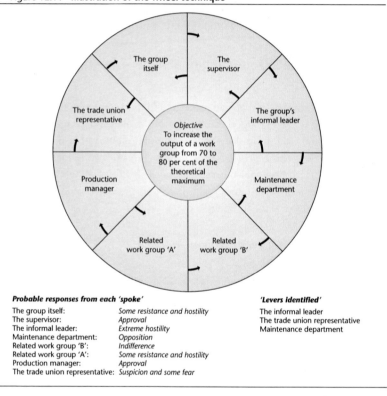

Probable responses from each 'spoke'

The group itself:	*Some resistance and hostility*
The supervisor:	*Approval*
The informal leader:	*Extreme hostility*
Maintenance department:	*Opposition*
Related work group 'B':	*Indifference*
Related work group 'A':	*Some resistance and hostility*
Production manager:	*Approval*
The trade union representative:	*Suspicion and some fear*

'Levers identified'

The informal leader
The trade union representative
Maintenance department

5   Look again at your objectives and outcomes:

- Describe in as much detail as possible the situation when the objective is achieved. Include in this the time-scales required for accomplishment.

- Ask yourself if the objectives and outcomes are still realistic. Do you have any doubts? Can you take any further actions to make your objectives more realistic?

6   Review the various players you have identified in each 'spoke' of your wheel and consider their possible response to the changes. At this stage simply indicate in broad terms their expected reaction: will they approve, oppose, or be indifferent to the changes?

7   Look out for the 'levers' of change:

- In any 'spoke' there may be one or several individuals who have some power to influence either positively or negatively the desired change.

- Such individuals might be considered as potential 'levers' of change. In some cases these people may perform relatively simple roles in the organisation, but they might be invested with power in this situation because of the nature of the change involved – for example, a manager who leans heavily on the advice of his personal assistant, or a production operator whose co-operation is essential if documents are to be printed and distributed on time.

- It is crucial that you talk to these people to assess their views on the proposed changes. They may also be able to provide you with information on other interested parties.

8   Prioritise the 'spokes'. Think about which groups or individuals may be able to influence other 'spokes'. Equally, identify those spokes that are likely to offer maximum support and opposition to the changes.

9   Consider the inter-relationship between each 'spoke'. Does this provide additional insights into the power relationships? Does it provide you with alternative influencing strategies to lobby for the changes?

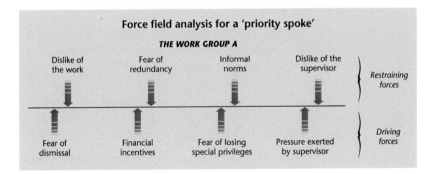

Force field analysis for a 'priority spoke'

10   Do a force field analysis of each spoke or stakeholder (see p. 174). Review your priority list of 'spokes' and then conduct an analysis of the various driving and restraining forces in each priority 'spoke'. To do this:

- Take a piece of paper and draw a horizontal line across the middle to represent the equilibrium position. Then list what you consider to be the factors that will drive or slow down that spoke in relation to the proposed changes.

- The driving forces are the arguments and factors that will work in favour of the change.

- The restraining forces are those arguments and factors that will hinder or prevent the change taking place.

- Clearly you are basing your assessment on a combination of facts and impressions, so you will be exercising an element of judgement in detailing the actual factors.

- Try to estimate the relative importance of each of the restraining forces by giving each a score between 1 (low impact) and 10 (high impact).

11 Devise *action plans to* help leverage the driving forces for the change and at the same time to remove or minimise the restraining forces.

- You can now design a comprehensive strategy for managing the stakeholder side of the change. In so doing you will have taken account of all the key groups and people involved, and the type of support and resistance they are likely to offer.

- It is preferable to either remove or minimise the restraining forces than to simply rely on the strength of the driving forces. If you do the latter, you may achieve your objective, but the cost may be a higher level of resistance from people who felt their issues were ignored.

- Overall, the strategy for increasing or adding to the list of driving forces should succeed because management will work hard at it. But by applying pressure and removing people who resist you also create resistance which might prove more costly to the organisation in the long run. In change processes, strong and proactive involvement usually generate higher levels of commitment and ownership. This means that any changes will take hold.

- Remember that the process of removing or reducing the restraining forces may take a long time in the case of major organisational and cultural change. This is the real challenge in introducing complex change. There are no easy ways of overcoming a person's sense of damaged pride, or possible loss of status or autonomy.

12 A note of caution

The 'wheel technique' represents just one perspective of the situation. There is plenty of scope for getting your assessment wrong. You can never be sure that you have correctly identified or assessed all the key stakeholders. Even if your 'wheel' and force-field analyses are detailed and accurate, remember that the situation can always change.

Corporate communications

An essential element of a high performance organisation is having effective communications at all staff levels. In some ways communications is a barometer of how well an organisation functions. In particular, the ability of senior managers to communicate effectively with their staff is often a sign of a healthy or unhealthy organisation. Companies that communicate with and involve people fully in the business are rewarded with a motivated and committed workforce that supports and implements strategies with greater force and vigour. So good organisations spend considerable amounts of time and effort fine-tuning their communications processes.

A review of the major challenges facing organisations today shows how important communications is to engaging people. Some of these challenges are immensely complex, and the messages needed to deal with them require considered thought:

- geo-political uncertainty
- volatile capital markets
- the threat of global terrorism
- globalisation of markets and industries
- relentless competition and downward cost pressure
- the rise of anti-consumer and anti-capitalism protest groups
- increased regulatory regimes
- continued advancements in technology/internet/communications
- increased environmental pressure
- increasing legal action by consumers against corporations and their products and services
- less loyal customers
- the need for constant changes in business direction and structure
- the need for greater people flexibility and efficiency.

On a more tactical level, it is important when formulating corporate communications to be clear about the message you are trying to communicate. Managers often overcomplicate matters and a message loses its impact because it is not understood. Keep messages clear and simple rather than elaborate and detailed. Think in terms of the list of three. Research indicates that there is something about the human brain that makes it easier for people to recall messages or information that consist of lists of three as opposed to eight or ten. By detailing the three key factors necessary to turn the business around you increase the likelihood that the message will be remembered.

Figure 12.12 **Effective communications**

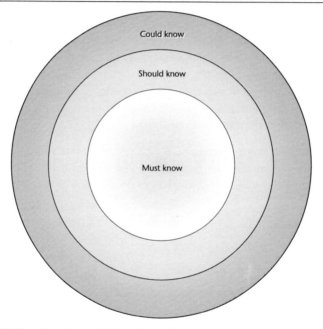

MUST KNOWS: *Vital points:* profitability; business performance; local/team news; unit performance; health and safety
SHOULD KNOWS: *Desirable but not essential:* changes in senior management; competitor performance; future product development
COULD KNOWS: *Relatively unimportant*

It is also important when developing a communications strategy that you are clear about what you want the message to achieve. Think about the possible outcomes you are seeking to achieve:

* inform about new developments

* instruct on the new way

* persuade or convince people

- negotiate a way forward

- advise people about the latest developments or future proposals

- establish standards or discipline

- challenge existing thinking or perceptions

- motivate people to support a proposal or overcome a challenge

- build a team

- involve people in a discussion or proposal

- inquire about peoples' views on an issue.

Having a clear outcome in mind prevents confused messages being given. If you are clear about what you are trying to achieve you increase the likelihood that you will do so. Also bear in mind that people primarily want to know about matters that will have an impact on them and their day-to-day work. Too often corporate communications fail because they are viewed as being too distant or irrelevant to the people receiving them. Check and audit any information that is communicated to staff against the following set of criteria:

- Is it accurate?

- Is it clear and understandable?

- Is it relevant and meaningful to the person?

- Is it the right time to be giving the message or information?

- Is the information source reliable?

- Is the information credible?

When you are deciding on information to include in a corporate message, consider it against the following criteria:

- They *must know* this information – it is absolutely crucial that they have this data to perform or implement something.

- They *should know* this information – it is desirable that people are aware of this information as it will help them in their daily work.

- They *could know* this information – it is not critical and it will not create any problems or difficulties if people are not aware of the information.

Making use of communications channels – and the rise of email

The first thing an army does when it goes to war is to attack the enemy's communications systems. It tries to destroy the central command posts and communications centres as fast as possible. Managing communications in times of change is akin to fighting a battle. If you are trying to implement a new policy, organisation structure or business plan, or to merge with another business, you must win the communications war. Many organisations now recognise the need to involve staff in their business and to encourage them to provide ideas and suggestions to improve performance. In terms of the communication channels available to managers, the choice has never been greater. Since the first edition of this book we have witnessed the revolution and some might now say cancer of email. At its best email can democratise a workplace and dramatically transform communications in a business. At its worst it can make an organisation and its managers grind to a halt. Some businesses clearly have problems with unlimited amounts of email. Aided by poor training and corporate disciplines, email and wider internet abuse is felt to be widespread in many companies. In some cases it might be said to have replaced many of the older and more established means of communications.

Some of the classic communications channels that may need to be managed are:

- corporate or office notice boards – more often web-based
- weekly bulletin sheets or newsletters – now more likely to reside in the email box and left unread
- staff handbooks – now mostly moved to the web
- formal team briefings
- informal staff discussions
- corporate videos – now rapidly being replaced by webcasts and videoconferencing
- top team briefings
- staff meetings
- company journals or magazines – increasingly moved to the web
- trade unions
- external media – press and TV, including web-based ones
- social network sites as well as the traditional staff grapevine.

When considering the use of these, always remember that the message is more important than the medium. In the past many expensive corporate videos have failed because the medium appeared more important than the message. Despite the advances of email and social networking, the grapevine and face-to-face communication remain the most powerful forms of communication in most organisations. The speed with which a message is delivered is also an important part of the process. There is little point in communicating something that most people already know about. The rise of email and networking sites has of course helped spread and supplement the power of the grapevine, and they are now almost impossible to beat for speed. While acknowledging the role of the grapevine, people often distrust its accuracy – they know it is important but that it also has limitations. In the majority of cases, people still prefer to get their information direct from management, and have the opportunity to question management over an issue.

Another important development in communications is the electronic record or footprint that email creates. This resulted in embarrassment for some Wall Street investment bankers who were caught up in the mis-selling of products and services scandals of the late 1990s. It is also coming to prominence in individual cases of discrimination and misconduct, whereby email trails reveal examples of managerial abuse or misconduct. As a result, corporations are tightening their email protocols, rules and standards.

Despite the great advantages email offers in being able to move information and messages quickly, face-to-face briefings and discussions between managers and staff are probably still the most effective means of communication. Even so, the success of such briefings relies heavily upon the quality of the information and the message being given. When reviewing communications, managers should audit their approach against the areas identified in Figure 12.13. These encompass the objective, message, structure, channels, skills required and people involved.

Figure 12.13 **Reviewing communications effectiveness**

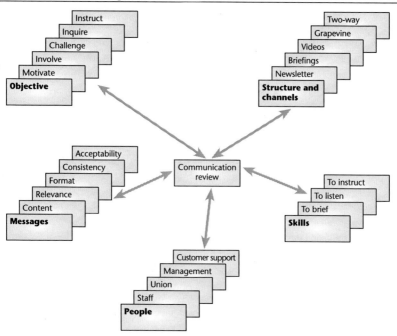

Some organisations will have special operational pressures and problems that may require even more bespoke approaches. Shiftworking and other anti-social hours can cause special problems in trying to get a consistent and speedy message across to employees. Extra care needs to be applied in such situations.

Managing performance – a core people management process

Few organisational activities create more emotion, worry or confusion than the annual round of performance reviews and appraisals. This is a big missed opportunity, because in many organisations the performance management process can be a key driver for overall business performance. When implemented effectively it can also be an extremely helpful and positive activity that promotes powerful working relationships.

Figure 12.14 Business and people performance linkages

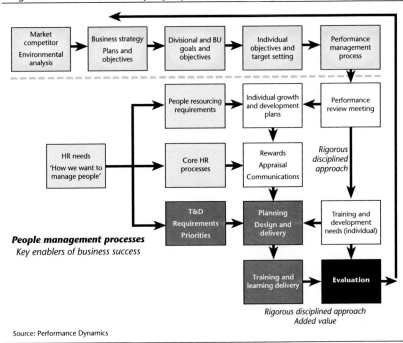

People management processes
Key enablers of business success

Rigorous disciplined approach
Added value

Source: Performance Dynamics

So why is there so often a negative reaction to the performance management cycle? Too often in organisations an HR function will have designed a form or procedure, issued it and announced: 'From the first of next month, there will a regular performance review process installed.' The result is no real understanding or commitment to the process. The exercise is often seen as a bureaucratic process that does little to support the business. In addition, managers see the process as overly complex and bureaucratic.

In high performance organisations the performance management process will have been designed and developed with the key people involved. The logic and business rationale surrounding the process will have been debated and explained. Any worries or concerns will have been recognised and dealt with. Everyone involved will be aware of the purpose of the activity: to provide an opportunity for the individuals and their managers to review how well they are meeting the business needs, now and in the future. The bigger and more significant objective is to align individual objectives with the overall business strategy. Figure 12.14 shows how this linkage works and how the performance management process feeds into other core HR processes.

Why have a performance management process?

The effective performance of people in an organisation depends on being able to match an individual's knowledge, skills and motivation to their current and future role. This role should of course be making a real contribution to driving the overall business strategy. A major part of any manager's job is to manage individual performance and to assess whether people are performing well and whether additional support, guidance or coaching is needed. At all times a manager should be driving staff towards delivering objectives that support the overall business plan. At the same time, any employee has their own needs in terms of rewards, growth, ambition and development that must be aligned. To succeed in balancing these needs, both manager and employee need to provide each other with clear goals and feedback.

Although some managers work with their staff on a daily basis, the performance management process instils a formal discipline of taking time away from the day-to-day pressures to check on mutual needs and to provide feedback and guidance in a constructive and disciplined way.

A good performance review process deals with questions such as:

- What am I doing right in the role – what are my strengths?
- What am I doing wrong – what development needs do I have?
- What can I do better or improve on?
- What do I need to stop doing?
- What help or support do I need from my manager?

Any feedback from a manager to a staff member needs to be based on real evidence if it is to be useful. The focus of a performance review needs to be on job performance and real outcomes rather than personality characteristics.

The benefits for both the individual and the organisation include the following:

Individual

- is made fully aware of the manager's and organisation's assessment
- the reasons for both success and failure are analysed and agreed
- any improvement actions and targets are identified and agreed
- any training and development needs are identified and agreed
- future job plans and prospects are discussed
- other development opportunities are discussed
- the individual is able to voice any other relevant issues or concerns.

Organisation

- the effectiveness of past recruitment and selection procedures can be assessed
- future talent can be identified – including high potentials
- future learning and development programmes can be designed by collating individual performance review discussions
- past and future promotion or development decisions can be made and evaluated
- the development of future business plans can be aided by important talent availability discussions
- information for rewards policy and decision-making.

Conducting a performance management meeting

A checklist of good management practice

Planning and preparation

1. Review your colleague's performance well in advance of the meeting
2. Identify some key issues from your managerial perspective
3. Identify the positive as well as the development issues
4. Rehearse any negative feedback – apply negative feedback rules – be specific and provide real examples
5. Prepare some simple notes to help keep you on track during the discussion
6. Agree a suitable meeting time – avoid particularly pressurised days
7. Set sufficient time aside – one or two hours
8. Get in the right frame of mind – positive, opportunity to discuss teamwork and development, and so on
9. Opportunity to give positive feedback
10. Recognise it's an important if not urgent activity that most people enjoy

The meeting – introduction

1. Shut off calls, action do not disturb instructions, and so on

2   Get into the right frame of mind – focused, positive and relaxed

3   Be clear about the issues you would like to explore as the manager

4   Welcome and thank your colleague for their time and the opportunity to meet

5   Confirm and set out the purpose and timing of the meeting

6   Emphasise that the focus of the discussion is on development and improving the effectiveness of how we all work together – desire to improve teamwork and so on across business

7   Highlight any competences that the colleague is assessed against – models of effective behaviours and skills – again stress the business objective of raising our corporate-wide skills and capability

8   Stress that the session is about development as well as an appraisal process – need to discuss individual and unit business objectives, career planning, and so on

9   Emphasise the confidentiality of the discussion

10   Stress your desire for openness and a quality discussion

11   Highlight the outcomes of the discussion – agreement on some actions – personal development plan

12   Check that your colleague is happy with the objectives and purpose

The meeting – the feedback discussion

1   Set out some key principles first

- need to maintain a balance on the positive feedback as well as any negatives

- want to promote strengths as well as identify any improvement areas

2   Stress your desire to get your colleague's reactions and views and to discuss and explore the various issues together

3   Begin by asking your colleague for their view of their performance:

- What do you think about your contribution and performance?

4   Focus the first part of the discussion on the strengths of the person:

- What do you see as your positives and strengths

5   Keep the energy focused on your colleague by using a series of probing comments and questions to get them to give you their interpretation of the feedback:

- Oh ... could you say a little bit more as to why you think that?

- So that surprised you?

- Have there been any other surprises?

- What specifically do you consider your strengths?

- Why do you think that might be an issue?

- So you were pleased with that?

- Do you think you are prone to act in that way at times?

6   Avoid diving in or taking the lead in the discussion
    - keep the energy with your colleague

    - listen and remember you do not have to do all the talking

7   Apply the 80–20 principle in the conversation – you should be talking for only 20% of the time

8   Get agreement on the strengths and development issues before moving on to discuss possible solutions

9   Offer your views but speak for yourself not others
    - use 'I' – 'I do sometimes see you being too detail focused'

    - avoid 'It has been reported or commented on that' type comments

10 Build on the themes being voiced by your colleague and develop the discussion
    - avoid jumping to new topics or issues too quickly

    - see it as a conversation rather than a heavily driven agenda

11 Ask your colleague to summarise the feedback and discussion
    - 'So what is this all telling you in terms of your strengths and areas to work on?'

12 Add your own managerial perspective and opinions
    - 'I would like you to be more participative in the project planning'

    - 'Yes I think you could do more of . . . and less of . . .' But be specific.

13 Get agreement to the conclusions before beginning to explore possible action plans and a development plan

The meeting close

14 Consider the 'Stop, Start and Continue' structure and explore lots of options not just formal training

15 Consider on the job experiences, coaching with a colleague, self study, change of responsibilities, new tasks to help develop skills, regular review sessions, secondments, and so on

16 As the manager offer suggestions and guidance but don't dictate
  * ensure your colleague is committed before agreeing to any actions
  * your colleague should own any solutions, not you

17 Agree the actions and commit them to writing
  * be specific
  * to do what by when and to what standard

18 Confirm review periods to follow up
  * invite any final comments and thank your colleague for their time

People and organisation capability in your organisation

The following checklists present some questions that may prove helpful to assess an organisation's overall capability.

No checklist can be exhaustive, so treat them as open-ended. Use them to provoke thought and to stimulate discussion. They will help you to identify the crucial people and organisation issues facing your organisation.

The aim of the analysis is to explore how a considered and planned approach to people management can help improve business performance.

Business strategy and human resources management

'Organisation panic points' checklist

Warning signs of an organisation in trouble: Do you have any of these problems?

* loss of market share
* low levels of productivity
* slow speed to market capabilities
* increasing costs
* poor cash flow
* lack of new product or service innovation
* increasing levels of customer complaint
* poor employee relations
* increasing or erratic levels of staff turnover

- evidence of poor quality and service
- excessive evidence of top team conflicts and disagreements
- dissatisfaction with rewards and the general level of employee conditions
- lack of clear job roles and responsibilities
- no clear performance measures
- erratic or poor product service/delivery records
- poor recruitment standards/practices
- little evidence of staff development and continued learning
- no induction training for new employees
- business experiences critical skills shortages
- evidence of excessive organisational politics and departmental conflicts.

Culture, organisation, people, systems (COPS) analysis

Culture
- Do staff identify with the organisation and do they see the success of the organisation as being of direct benefit to themselves?
- Do staff see themselves as having common interests with their work colleagues and group? Is there a strong team spirit?
- Is work allocated on the basis of individual expertise rather than position in the organisation?
- Are staff encouraged to say what they think about the organisation?
- Does the organisation encourage innovation and creativity among staff?
- Do staff feel a sense of personal responsibility for their work?
- Is quality emphasised in all aspects of the organisation?

Organisation
- Does the structure of the organisation encourage effective performance?
- Is the organisation structure flexible in the face of changing demands?
- Is the structure too complex? If so, in what areas?
- Do staff have clear roles and responsibilities?
- Does the organisation structure push problems up rather than resolve them at the point where they occur?
- Do procedures and management practices facilitate the accomplishment of tasks?

- Do you constantly seek to challenge your organisation structure?
- Do people have narrow or wide job definitions?

People

- Do staff have the necessary skills and knowledge to perform their jobs in the most effective manner?
- Do staff understand their jobs and how they contribute to overall business performance?
- Do staff have a customer service orientation?
- Are people with potential identified and developed for the future?
- Are staff encouraged to perform well through the giving of recognition, feedback, and so on?
- Do people know what their expected performance standards are?

Systems (HR)

- Do the organisation's HR systems (for example, recruitment, promotion, planning, management, information and rewards) encourage effective performance among your staff?
- Are these systems consistent across the organisation?
- Are there clear rewards for effective performance within your work group?
- Does the organisation review its systems frequently and ensure they mutually support each other?

Consider:

1   What are the three critical people issues facing your business?
    - (1)
    - (2)
    - (3)
2   What plans/actions are you taking to address them?
3   What are your timescales?
4   What additional resources do you need?

Identifying training needs – a management guide

An employee in your team, division or organisation is not performing as well as they should. How can you begin to define what the problem is? Ask yourself some of these basic questions. They help review all aspects of the problem and will lead you to the right conclusion.

1   Why is the work performance unsatisfactory?

  •   What events or problems cause you to say things are not right?

  •   Are you clear what the individual should be doing and what standards of performance they should be meeting?

  •   Be clear on the specifics in relation to non-performance – collect real examples – deal in facts not opinions.

2   On a more radical note, have you considered whether the role or job would be better carried out in some other way?

  •   Is it possible to change the way the job is performed?

  •   Would you be allowed to effect such a change?

  •   What do you have to do to change it?

If a change in performance is necessary, consider the following questions. Try to identify whether the problem is related to the way the work is being carried out (is it a skill issue?) or whether it is related to the attitude of the individual. In some cases the two may be linked, but you need to identify what is causing the problem in the first place before you can solve it.

First, consider the problem as being 'related to the way the work is carried out':

  •   Is the work rewarding the individual in some way for achieving performance?

  •   Does the individual consider that delivering the desired performance requires 'too much effort for insufficient reward'?

  •   What rewards or satisfaction (for example, pay, bonuses, prestige, spare time) does the individual receive as a result of their present effort or the desired performance level?

  •   Are you rewarding irrelevant behaviours and overlooking others that may be more critical to delivering increased performance?

  •   Can you change the rewards system to help change behaviours?

  •   Is the individual able to demonstrate competence in the required task?

  •   Is there evidence that the individual lacks the skill required to perform the task?

  •   Would some form of retraining or learning be needed to help address the problem?

- What training might be recommended to address the performance issue?

- If the individual does not develop the required skills, what are the consequences? Can the individual be allowed to function without this skill?

- Are there any other obstacles to further skills development?

- Does the individual know what is expected of them in terms of performance and delivery?

- Does the individual lack the authority, time or resources to complete the work in the desired manner?

- Is there a 'right way of doing it' or the 'way that it has always been done' that might be changed?

- If it is a resourcing or time problem, can you reduce the demands of less important tasks or problems to free up time?

Now consider the performance problem as being *'personal to the individual'*:

- Does the individual have the ability to do the work required?

- What are the competences and skills necessary to do the job?

- Has the individual previously performed the role effectively?

- Has the job changed in some way?

- Is feedback provided about how the job should be done?

- Does the individual have to perform this particular task or use the skill on a regular basis?

- Would more practice help the individual in developing their capability?

- Is there a positive attitude to getting the job done and to developing a solution to the performance difficulties?

- Is there evidence of any attitudinal change in the individual involved?

- Are any needs or personal issues affecting the individual's performance – problems at home, family illness, and so on?

Having completed the analysis, what should you do next? Here are some final-summary questions to reflect on before deciding your plan of action.

- Is the individual willing to assist in finding a solution? Is there real evidence of a motivational problem? In such cases you may need to counsel the individual rather than pursue the training route. Investing in training will not overcome any motivational problems that arise from issues outside work.

- What solution will require the most or least effort? There is little point in investing huge amounts of effort in minor problems. But if you are dealing with a key performer in a crucial role you need to get to the root of the problem.

- What solution is most likely to succeed in addressing the performance issue? Be clear about the solution – consider retraining, placing alongside a high performer or additional coaching.

- What solution are you best equipped to implement? Implement what is appropriate and within your available resources.

- Is it worth the investment? What will it 'cost' to solve the problem and what will be the benefits if you succeed?

13 Competitive marketing strategy

The purpose of strategy

A successful marketing strategy is fundamental to a company's ability both to market and develop its products or services successfully and to build and maintain increased profitability.

To achieve its objectives a company needs above all to be aware of where it stands in relation to both its customers and its competitors – hence the title of this chapter.

Although the concept of strategy is frequently misunderstood and constantly redefined, it would be difficult to argue with Professor Gary Hamel's comment that 'strategy is, above all else, the search for above average returns'.

This section suggests that strategy is *not*:

- a plan to produce 20 per cent growth in earnings per share
  - this is a by-product of successful strategy
- a decision to divest under-performing assets or product lines
  - this is an action which frees up resources to allow strategy to be pursued in other areas, such as expansion of a high-potential export market.

Acquisitions and divestments themselves do not represent strategy, although they may result from a clearly thought-out strategy. Strategy *is*:

- selecting markets and market segments in which to compete
- providing a mix of products and services that customers value
- doing it all better – or for lower cost – than your competitors.

It is the interaction of customer *needs* and competitive *offerings and costs* which determines:

- who makes the sale, and
- and at what profit.

The essence of strategy is to identify the business areas in which you can achieve a competitive edge. Why is concentration on competitive edge so important? It is not just a question of offering a better product or service, or even offering these at a lower price. You also need to provide this extra value to your customers at a cost which will result in profit. This may sound obvious, but is often not focused on clearly enough.

It is also necessary to build a strategic competitive advantage in order to maintain a differential edge. IBM's competitive advantage, for example, was its much-vaunted ability to solve all sorts of computer-related problems. It could do this because it had successfully established the type of technical, service and distribution resources required – in other words, the structure was in place.

Michael Porter, author of the classic *Competitive Strategy: techniques for analysing industries and competitors*, says that competitive strategy is about being different, but he also says that a company will outperform its rivals only if it can establish a difference that it can preserve.

Porter established three sources of competitive advantage: lowest cost, differentiation and focus. He now talks about 'the two basic forms of competitive advantage: cost leadership and differentiation'. Today, however, it might be said that one or other is insufficient and that companies need to establish clear cost leadership and differentiation.

Ikea offers low-cost furniture with high design and production values. It is instantly available, you take it away, you assemble it yourself. You can shop during long opening hours and your children can enjoy play areas while you select. Convenience, style, affordability.

Porter's 'Five Forces' model clarifies the ways in which some markets are more attractive than others, not only to you but to your competitors as well. Remember that your competitors will be looking at this model in relation to your best markets. The five forces are:

- Rivalry among existing competitors – how strong are their brands, what is their market share? How will this affect your own need for marketing spend and price reduction?

- Ease of entry or threat of entry from new competitors – how easy or difficult are the entry barriers?

- Substitutes – how many and how good? How will that affect your prices and profitability?

- Bargaining power of buyers – customers buying from retailers, retailers from suppliers. How will this affect margins?

- Bargaining power of suppliers – suppliers of raw materials selling to manufacturers, manufacturers supplying retailers. Again, how will this affect margins at different stages of the chain?

To identify those areas of growth where you can best build and match your competitive advantage to your customers' needs, you need to:

- think of planning in competitive, relative terms

- ask yourself, when looking at market growth, not just *what* has happened but *why?*

Think about a particular product or service in your own business.

- What has driven its growth?

- What is going to happen next?

A classic example occurred in the 1960s, when the Japanese successfully anticipated the need to replace the 1940s-built cargo ships still being used by most industrialised countries. They were first to fill this market need, and then moved into the more profitable business of building oil tankers.

Now list – in order of importance – your own customers' criteria for buying your product or service, for example:

- availability

- reliability

- price

- service

- ease of purchase, for example online

- technical specification

- identity/brand.

You can then draw various conclusions. For example, recent research into the purchase criteria employed in the control and instrumentation industry showed that:

- technical back-up was seen as very important for large products, but not at all for small ones

- price was important for wholesalers of small products but less so for their end-users

- delivery speed was crucial for users of small products and almost immaterial for large ones.

Remember when conducting research to:

1   be sure that your sample is a good cross-section

2   structure your questions properly to ensure that you find out what
    your customers really think.

Market segments: from sharks to piranhas

Sometimes differing demands will emerge within the same market – it may
have split into more than one or segmented. If you have a cluster of people
with a significantly different set of demands, that is a segment.

How can you supply your product or service better than your competitors,
and at a lower cost, for differing sets of needs and requirements? The answer
is to establish a niche marketing strategy. Build your competitive advantage
in a specific segment; in other words, become a piranha, not a shark.

There are myriad customer needs. Creating fresh segments (finding particular
groups, particular needs) can be a test of your own creativity.

Go back to your own customers' *key purchasing criteria*. Now break down your
market into two segments and work out how the criteria will vary in each.

For example, a manufacturer of outside camera mounting equipment segments
its market into professional and amateur:

Rating	Professional
1	Weight
2	Technical performance
4	Availability
3	Quality/reliability
5	Price

Rating	Amateur
4	Weight
5	Technical performance
2	Availability
3	Quality/reliability
1	Price

If the manufacturer gets weight and technical performance right, it will clearly
win in the professional market, but not in the amateur market, where price and
availability are the key factors.

Another way of looking at the competition is to weight your list of key purchase criteria (which you will have established through your research) and then allocate points to yourself and your competitor under each heading.

Here is another example from the house building industry:

Weighted criteria	Us	Them	Weighting [total 100]
1 Price	6	8	35
2 Delivery/programme	9	8	25
3 Technical service	8	9	20
4 Technical specification	9	8	15
5 Quality assurance	10	6	5

What is happening here? The competition is winning market share through scoring higher on the key criterion of price.

The first rule of strategy is 'Know your adversary'. It is not enough to know what your customers want and which aspects of your product or service they value most highly. You also need to know all about your competition. If you know

1   what your customers want, and

2   what your competitors are offering

You will then know

3   which competitor/product is growing/declining.

Any two of these will give you the other piece of information.

It is always important to compare competitor ratings for key purchase criteria to gain a clear picture of your competitors':

* marketing strategy

* chances of growing or declining in the market.

You should measure your competitor's response/performance in relation to various key purchase criteria, such as delivery, service, price, quality, technical support, credit, availability, and so on.

In comparing competitor ratings, your analysis might, for example, reveal the following.

* Competitor A goes for a 'pile 'em high, sell 'em cheap' policy. Availability is not particularly good, but quality is reasonable. It survives on price advantage alone.

- Competitor B takes an approach based on reliability and scores consistently well, especially on quality. It's by no means the cheapest, but it doesn't have to be, because of its sound reputation.

- Competitor C goes for the highest quality in terms of service and technical support, and easily beats the rest of the field. It has a clear competitive edge in these two key areas.

- Competitor D is stuck in the middle, trying to do everything and not scoring significantly in any area. It's in trouble.

What do you do if price is a major criterion and you are being beaten?

- examine your costs and pricing structure

- if you cannot reduce costs or do not choose to, look at where you can add value.

This is a situation where you may well have to test your creativity in finding a new segment where price is not the key factor. But note that it may not be possible to attack a new segment without putting fresh strain on existing resources, such as technical, production, promotion or distribution. In this case, think again. First decide how you wish to segment the market in question and which criteria to use. You can construct a simple set of criteria or a more complex set of variables, depending on the situation.

Typical criteria would be as follows:

- **Demographic**
  - age
  - sex
  - occupation
  - income
  - education
  - socioeconomic group (A, B, C1, C2, and so on)

- **Customer behaviour**
  - usage (non-user, light/heavy user)
  - benefits sought (economy, status)
  - marketing factor sensitivity (quality, price, service)
  - preferred marketing channel (online or 'bricks and mortar' retail)

- **Geographic**
  - region
  - density (urban, rural)

- **Behavioural**
    - political (radical, conservative, liberal)
    - social (assertive, non-assertive)
    - ambition (ambitious striver, low achiever)
    - autonomy (dependent, independent)

These variables are only some examples of the many criteria you can use. They may or may not be important, but the exercise of thinking through which variables matter is in itself of great value. It can also be creative, in establishing a potential new market segment.

- It is up to you which criteria you select; these will vary depending on the product or markets.

- There may be little or no segmentation under certain main headings (such as geographic) and a great deal of segmentation within others (such as benefits sought).

- Be consistent in your research, namely the questions you ask.

- Always ensure you take a representative sample. Re-check your assumptions through further research, perhaps via your salesforce.

Costs and market share

The experience curve

A great deal has been written about business strategy in a competitive marketing context. Theories of market share and new product development have been invented and refined. In essence, the classic theory is:

- market share relative to the competition helps to create scale – this is known as the 'experience curve'

- the 'experience curve' reduces costs

- market share is therefore the key to increased profits.

Put another way, costs are a function of accumulated volume; high market share can yield low costs and high profits; and products should be managed differently, as a function of their relative market share and market growth, to achieve high product/market shares relative to the competition (see Figure 13.1).

Remember when dealing with market share:

1   It is important to be very clear about which market or markets you are talking about.

2   The key words are 'relative to the competition', that is, your volume, your costs and your pricing are a function of the *realisable* market in relation to your competition.

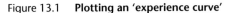

Figure 13.1   **Plotting an 'experience curve'**

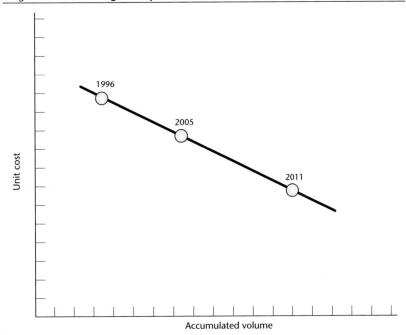

As Bruce Henderson, founder of the Boston Consulting Group, wrote: 'Strategic sectors are defined entirely in terms of competitive differences. Market share in the strategic sector, not size of company, is what determines profitability.'

The product portfolio

The theory goes on to say that products should be managed differently – especially from an investment point of view – depending on where they stand in relation to:

*   relative market share

*   market growth.

Figure 13.2   **The 'Boston matrix'**

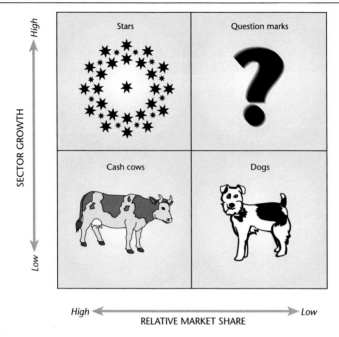

Out of this theory emerged the now famous 'Boston matrix' (see Figure 13.2), which graphically demonstrates the relative position of a group of products within a company. It introduced a menagerie of terms: stars, cash cows, dogs and question marks.

- *Stars*: high relative market share, in a growing market – likely to need further investment.

- *Cash cows*: dominant market position in a declining or static market – needs careful maintenance.

- *Dogs*: little or no sector growth, and no real market share – disinvest.

- *Question marks*: low market share in an expanding market creates the problem child – rethink.

The matrix is divided simply into four; you can subdivide it further by breaking down each side into, say, ten units. This will give you a more refined view. For example, one of your stars might be nearer the centre in terms of both sector growth and relative market share – the investment decision is then not so simple. Generally, though, this is a simple and effective matrix to clarify initial thinking on product portfolios.

- Don't overinvest in your stars. Put in whatever is necessary to sustain growth.

- Don't overwork your cash cows – don't just milk them and starve them of fresh promotional support.

- Problems thrown up by dogs and question marks – even cash cows for that matter – might well be solved by further thought on fresh market segmentation strategies.

Figure 13.3   **Product life cycle illustrations**

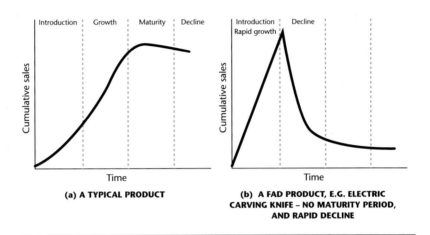

(a) A TYPICAL PRODUCT

(b) A FAD PRODUCT, E.G. ELECTRIC CARVING KNIFE – NO MATURITY PERIOD, AND RAPID DECLINE

The product life cycle

The product life cycle (see Figure 13.3) forms a key part of traditional business strategy. Quite simply, it traces the volume and rate of growth of a product over time.

Watch out for the period required for demand for replacement product to come through. That is, beware of market saturation and be concerned about replacement product as well as market penetration.

Don't look just for growth and market share, but for sustainable market share. The 'experience curve' shows that as a company gains experience in manufacturing a product, costs decline further. It is all a matter of scale.

The experience of Honda and the development of the Japanese steel industry during the 1950s provide an interesting example:

- Japanese steel pours into the west

- manufactured steel prices in the west go up, in the east they go down
- Honda's product development progresses from construction to ships to cars, with further development via motorcycles and cars to pumps, outboard motors and lawnmowers.

Revenues and costs: the activity-based approach

The overall objective is always to maximise the difference between revenues and expenses. But it is possible to go further in trying to establish the link between products, market share, costs and profits.

Previous thinking has been very product-based. We need to switch our attention to activity. Why?

- The product-based approach looks at different products in relation to their sales revenue and the market position which the firm enjoys.
- An activity-based approach looks at the activities involved within the firm, for example:
    - technology/design
    - production/components
    - salesforce
    - promotion expenditure
    - service/technical back-up.
- Some people assume that there is a separate 'experience curve' for each product in a company. This is invariably wrong: most companies are more complex, with products that are not independent in terms of activity or economics.

If you now show how the different activities in the business match with the firm's mix of product lines, you can use activity to gain cost advantage. You need to understand:

- your marketing position in the product or market segment you are in
- what is going on inside the firm
- where you are spending the money generated by the firm's activities
- whether the revenues you are creating will exceed those costs
- the growth rate of the activity in the workplace.

Remember:

- There is no such thing as a marketplace where costs don't matter.

- You're trying all the time to match your cost advantage with what one or more market segments require.

- It is important to maintain a clear picture of your costs compared with those of your competitors in relation to:
  - materials
  - labour
  - sales and marketing
  - distribution.

- A new area of business development may sound like a great marketing idea, but it may demand a significant change in activity levels. Is it still such a brilliant idea?

- Ask yourself:
  - what are my costs?
  - how do my competitors' costs differ in terms of:
    a) how they produce?
    b) what they produce?

What = design, specification (size, complexity, quality).

How = input costs, scale, efficiency, technology, location, tax/subsidies, distribution costs.

Establish a basis for analysing activity sharing within the firm. For example, look separately at your marketing and distribution activity:

1 Can the products or services you are offering share management and support personnel, as well as the same salesforce?

2 Can sales, advertising and promotion activity be directed at the same markets (and market segments), as well as through the same distribution channels?

3 Do a similar analysis of your distribution and service activities.

If you are looking at production and plant and process engineering, do the products share common components, suppliers, production facilities, personnel?

You should also draw up a comparison of activity structures among competing firms. Think about competitor cost comparison and work out who has built a significant cost advantage.

A typical cost comparison would compare:

- labour
- materials
- management overheads
- other fixed overheads
- transport
- research and development
- sales and administration
- your margin (revealing your cost advantage and/or price premium).

Remember that you do not have a good plan until you can say: 'Here is my cost advantage in providing this value to my market.'

Now write down the four (or more) main activities involved in your business. Then do the same for your main competitor. Estimate where you hold cost advantage, and where you don't.

Strategy formulation, planning and implementation

Deciding on a good strategy is not the result of a sudden flash of inspiration – it is a process. You need:

- data
- analysis
- ideas.

Break down your data into:

- market (size/growth, distribution structure, trends, trade)
- competitors (share/scale, growth, product/service offering, activities/integration, stated or apparent strategy)
- customers (who are they, what makes them buy, what trends are evident?)

You can find your data through a variety of sources:

- *internal* – what you know about customer needs, costs, and so on
- *indirect external* – government statistics, industry reports, and so on

- *direct external* – customer and competitor interviews.

Remember:

- It's better to be approximately right than precisely wrong.
- Don't get analysis paralysis.
- Don't let the numbers take over.

Analysis in strategy formulation should concentrate on:

- what is happening
  - segments and competitors
- why it is happening
  - product/service mix
- what it means for the bottom line
  - value-added activities
  - what drives the costs
- the alternatives
  - risk/return.

For ideas on strategy formulation, remember:

- Good ideas are rarely limited to one person. Go wide. Involve as many people as possible.
- Let strategy emerge slowly. Good ideas often filter back after several meetings and separate reflection.
- People enjoy talking about their ideas: listen carefully to what your organisation, the market place and other external sources are telling you.
- Encourage people to think through and express their own ideas.
- Tap into imagination as well as experience.
- Act: don't lose the momentum.

For the process of strategy formulation, remember:

- Don't try to get there in one go; a single meeting is rarely enough.
- Do go back, as fresh options emerge, to test your assumptions and re-work the data and analysis before finalising your strategy.
- Don't succumb to the 'short-cut disease'.

Last, these are the key points to remember for successful strategy implementation:

1 Be systematic, be patient and be thorough.

2 Note that strategy formulation is closely connected to strategy implementation.

3 Ensure that everybody understands what is involved; once the strategy is agreed you can then move rapidly to put it into action.

4 Make sure your operating plans link properly to your strategic plans; it's no good stating that 'we're going to be the sector's lowest-cost producer' while budgeting for high labour costs.

5 Beware of factors which can get in the way of implementation:

   * company culture
   * perceptions
   * habits
   * beliefs
   * morale
   * expectations
   * attitudes.

6 Draw up a schedule of the key tasks necessary for implementing your strategy, clarify responsibilities and set time limits.

7 Monitor progress.

There is nothing academic about the strategy formulation process: it must never be simply an intellectual exercise. It is there to be acted on.

Strategy that is well thought-out and implemented will feed through to the bottom line.

PART THREE

Business development

14 Strategy and business development

This chapter considers the best ways of developing an effective business strategy and then looks at the most crucial strategy-in-action area of how to approach the turnaround of a loss-making business.

A practical approach to developing a winning strategy

The ingredients needed to develop a winning strategy include:

- involving the whole senior management team to ensure mutual commitment
- adopting a rigorous and analytical approach
- spending sufficient time on formulating strategy – it must not be relegated to an item on a board meeting agenda.

When the strategy has been formulated, the next step is to translate it into a business plan and a budget for the next financial year. (Business plans are covered in Chapter 15, which should be regarded as complementary to this one.)

Effective strategic management

A business which practises effective strategic management will have:

- a one-page vision statement
- financial performance goals
- adequate financing
- defined key business development projects
- set strategic milestone of progress for the budget year
- created an effective organisational structure to implement the strategy
- adopted risk management
- used strategic management workshops.

Developing a strategy

The main elements to be addressed are:

- Assess trends and likely developments from:
    - economic background (for example, anticipated growth rates, currency developments, protectionism, tariffs)
    - political developments (for example, wider membership of European Union and other regional groups, the possible impact of a major terrorist attack, an armed conflict)
    - social trends (for example, population 'greying', major health issues such as swine flu or obesity)
    - consumerism (for example, greening of products, changing eating habits)
    - technology (for example, continued impact of internet, e-commerce, mobile telephony).
- Decide market segments, channels and countries to:
    - focus on
    - continue to develop
    - withdraw from.
- Evaluate opportunities for products and services to:
    - obtain market leadership
    - increase market share
    - create niche markets
    - be withdrawn if unprofitable.
- Monitor competitors continuously for:
    - products and services (for example, performance, design, service, innovation, pricing)
    - brand strength
    - distribution channel effectiveness
    - public relations success (for example, winning industry awards, valuable press coverage).
- Examine your existing business rigorously and critically:
    - role, effectiveness and cost of head and regional offices
    - product and service research, design, development and innovation to create distinctive benefits

- marketing and public relations

  - selling effectiveness and multi-channel selling

  - distribution channels

  - product or service production and delivery

  - after-sales service and regular customer or client contact

  - asset and working capital management

  - cost reduction opportunities

  - financial performance (gross profit, profit before tax, cash generation).

- Set financial performance goals:

  - listed companies (earnings per share growth, gearing level)

  - subsidiaries and private companies (profit growth, cash generation, return on new capital investment).

Important dimensions of strategy and business development:

These include:

- a vision statement

- a quantum leap approach

- taking stock of your marketplace and business

- identifying and evaluating the strategic options available

- organisation structure

- business development projects, with strategic milestones of progress

- the use of strategic workshops.

Each of these will be described.

Vision statement

Some managers regard a mission statement and a vision statement to be merely alternative names for the same thing, but they are markedly different.

A vision statement should describe the company, say, three or five years from now, and reflect the achievement of a quantum leap and the chosen strategic direction. To be meaningful, it requires the collective belief and commitment of the senior management team. The vision should harness and focus the energies of people to make it become a reality, setting priorities where appropriate. Ideally, the vision statement, which is a confidential company document, should be written on one side of one piece of paper.

In stark contrast, the majority of mission statements are merely a list of idealised corporate behaviour, such as product and service quality, customer care, equal opportunities, and so on. A mission statement for a consumer electronics manufacturer could well be swapped with that of a wealth management financial services company and be equally effective – or, in truth, equally ineffective.

Senior managers should remind themselves of their vision statement regularly to maintain their focus and commitment. The vision statements should include:

- the *market segments, channels and countries*
  - to achieve, maintain or enhance market leadership in
  - to continue investing in without achieving market leadership
  - to enter, by organic growth or acquisition as appropriate
  - to cut back, rationalise or exit from.

- the *commercial rationale of the company*
  - to describe how the company will be seen by customers and prospective customers as attractively and distinctively different from competitors, for example:
    a) all own-label products in our supermarkets will provide quality and specification comparable with the leading branded product at a lower price, or better quality at a lower price, or wherever possible an innovative product not available elsewhere and priced competitively
    b) our maintenance contract will include an annual dedicated software upgrade as part of the service.

- *essential policies and qualitative goals* which will be pursued, for example:
  - head office will act as investment banker and be as small as possible, and each subsidiary will be an autonomous business
  - sufficient investment will be made in information technology, or robotics, and so on to provide a competitive advantage in the marketplace compared with competitors
  - wherever possible, each member of staff will be rewarded by an incentive scheme based upon personal achievement.

- *broad financial-performance goals*, for example:
  - a minimum or average percentage increase in earnings per share each year

- the proportion of total profits to be achieved from a certain market within the next five years

- the percentage return to be achieved on total operating assets within five years.

- *future ownership* (this is particularly relevant for private companies and professional partnerships), for example:

  - a stockmarket listing will be obtained within the next three years

  - a merger with another partnership will be pursued to ensure that adequate technical support is affordable.

(These examples are from actual vision statements. This does not necessarily mean that they are appropriate for other companies to adopt.)

Copies of a business's vision statement should be restricted to directors, partners and senior executives because it is highly confidential. However, the relevant parts of the vision can be communicated orally to management and staff as part of briefing meetings. A vision statement is helpful in recruiting the most talented executives and technical specialists. Although it is not appropriate to provide a copy of the vision statement at the selection stage, reference to the vision will demonstrate that the company is committed to success.

Quantum leap approach

Belief in and commitment to the achievement of the vision are much more important for success than sophisticated corporate planning techniques. Aspiration and attitude are essential.

Some managers, however, simply plan to achieve mediocrity, and then do not manage to achieve even this. This is because they have planned for only a modest improvement in results, when this amounts to nothing more than continued mediocrity.

Outstanding managers are committed to achieving a quantum leap in results as a crucial part of the vision. A quantum leap is a dramatic improvement, without a significant increase in the commercial risks to be undertaken. Quantum leaps are not achieved in a week or a month, and probably not even in a year. Initiatives can be made during this week, this month and this year, however, which will result in a quantum leap being achieved within the medium term.

The ability to achieve a quantum leap is limited only by the imagination. The results achieved are more likely to fall short of the ambition than to exceed it. Imagination alone is not enough.

To achieve a quantum leap requires:

- *belief* – that it can and will be achieved

- *commitment* – to make the effort needed to make it happen

- *persistence* – to overcome setbacks and obstacles which will be encountered

- *enthusiasm* – to help motivate people.

The motto might be 'Think big and make it happen'. The growth and success of world-class companies did not happen by accident. The first step for a small business to become a national or world market leader is for the chief executive to have the vision, belief and total commitment to make it happen.

Taking stock

This means taking stock of present performance (comparing it with leading competitors where appropriate) and the market opportunities available. Objective measurement is needed; a comfortable view of performance seen through rose-tinted spectacles is inappropriate.

Facets of performance and market opportunities which should be assessed include:

- actual and forecast percentage market shares

- percentage share of each selling or distribution channel within a market

- attractive opportunities in different market segments and countries

- benefits and performance of each product or service group

- niche market opportunities which exist or could be created; for example, weekend hotel breaks to cater for special-interest groups such as those interested in gourmet food, wine tasting, antique collecting, bridge, clay-pigeon shooting

- gaps in the range of products or services offered

- overall percentage return on operating assets

- pricing and discount structures

- identification of major non-customers, especially in markets where there is a concentration of major customers such as supermarket groups and do-it-yourself superstore chains

- speed of delivery and the provision of after-sales service

- level of warranty claims or complaints, and the speed of handling them

- value of business lost by an inability to supply quickly enough

- opportunities to outsource service functions more cost effectively than providing them in-house, such as vehicle-fleet management, staff catering, pension administration, cleaning, physical distribution, specialist tax advice

- level of research and development expenditure, and the results achieved

- staff retention levels.

The aim of this assessment should be to identify:

- opportunities available within the existing business which should be capitalised upon

- attractive niche markets which can be created out of the existing business

- different market segments, channels and countries which should be entered

- the opportunity or need for selective price changes

- the need to set and to achieve improved standards of performance and to reduce costs.

Strategic options

A quantum leap in achievement requires that the strategic options are identified and evaluated. Furrow management, which is merely pursuing minor variations of the same theme, is the enemy of the quantum leap.

Strategic options need to be identified and evaluated for the overall business and within each major department. For example, strategic options at the corporate level of a listed company may include:

- acquiring a company overseas to achieve a significant local market share quickly

- obtaining a stockmarket listing in one or more overseas countries in which the company has a substantial business

- obtaining a separate stockmarket flotation for a major subsidiary (and retaining an equity stake), which would command a higher price-earnings ratio than the group as a whole

- transferring the freehold properties into a separate company and obtaining a stockmarket listing for it

- taking pre-emptive action to thwart a possible unwelcome bid.

Strategic options which should be evaluated to improve the marketing efforts of a professional partnership may include:

- recruiting a marketing director from outside the profession
- appointing a public relations consultancy to obtain press and magazine coverage
- presenting seminars to an invited audience of clients and prospective clients on subjects of topical interest that could create business opportunities
- inviting selected and prospective clients to lunch to discuss a subject related in some way to the services provided
- encouraging staff to write technical articles/blogs for publication in relevant magazines/websites
- experimenting with arts or sports sponsorship on a selective basis
- establishing personal contact with firms in different professions which are in a position to introduce business
- radically overhauling firm's website for ease of use and customer/client-useful information.

These examples are not recommendations for general use. The intention is to illustrate the range of strategic options which can be identified and evaluated in most business situations. Furrow management must be firmly rejected; this can be easily done by throwing away a self-imposed mental straitjacket.

Organisation structure

The organisation structure of a business is important for future success. The effect of organisation structure is rarely neutral. It is likely either to help the achievement of the vision, or to hamper progress and to encourage internal politics.

A problem is that organisational changes become necessary or desirable from time to time, so several piecemeal changes may be made to the structure over a period of time. As a result, the organisation structure should be reviewed comprehensively about every three years.

There is no such thing as an ideal organisation structure, not even within a particular industry. The organisation structure needs to be designed to help achieve the vision and to reflect the strategic options to be pursued.

Important features to be incorporated in an effective organisation structure include:

- clear definition of the role and added value of the head office or central management and the smallest number of people employed to achieve these
- individual businesses to serve particular market segments, rather than separate product or service groups, which may result in several subsidiaries serving, and even competing for, the same customer
- each business responsible for profit, with control of marketing and selling
- personal accountability for achieving measurable results throughout the business.

When the organisation structure has been redesigned to achieve the vision and strategic options selected, the strengths and weaknesses of key individuals should be taken into account. Some changes may be needed to capitalise on the strengths of certain people and to compensate for their weaknesses. The aim must be to produce an organisation structure that meets the business need and makes the best use of people. Occasionally, however, it may be necessary to recruit someone externally to fill a newly created key post rather than compromise by relying on candidates from within.

People talk about the loneliness of the chief executive of any business. An example of this is the creation of a new organisation structure. Involving members of the executive team in redesigning a new structure may cause problems arising from self-interest.

Organisation change often means that some people will gain in seniority and importance, while others will lose. If the chief executive of a business wants to involve other people, the choice should probably be restricted to the chairman, the group chief executive (where appropriate), the human resources director, non-executive directors or outside consultants to guard against vested interests and resistance to change.

Business development projects

Revolution spells danger for corporate success. In many businesses, with the severity of competition increasing faster than customer demand, evolution is likely to be equally dangerous. What is more, evolution alone is likely to be totally inadequate to achieve a quantum leap.

A proven way to drive a business forward is to create and vigorously pursue a handful of business development projects. Each project should be the specific responsibility of a member of the board or executive committee. Tangible milestones of achievement should be set to ensure adequate progress within the next 12 months. The capital expenditure, working capital and operating costs connected with each project should be included in the approved annual budget, to ensure that adequate resources are affordable and will be made available.

The business development projects should not be restricted to research and development. They should focus on whatever achievement is crucial to the achievement of the vision and a quantum leap. Projects could be concerned with any aspect of the business.

For example:

- entry into the US market by creating a regional office network

- a company-wide attack on quality, because sustained and critical media comment has seriously affected sales

- the launch of a major range of innovative healthy option and low-calorie convenience foods.

Some business development projects will be long term. They may address opportunities which rely upon future developments in advanced technologies such as artificial intelligence, biotechnology and next-generation mobile telephony. Nonetheless, milestones of progress need to be set and achieved within the next 12 months to ensure that the requisite urgency is maintained. In a business achieving only mediocre results, however, the business development projects are likely to focus more on short-term improvement.

Strategic workshops

Clearly, the structured approach to business development that has been described requires the commitment and involvement of every member of the board or executive committee. Strategic workshops are a powerful means to achieve this.

A strategic workshop should involve the board or executive committee of the business. The aim is to address those issues which are vital to future success. These could include the creation of a vision for success; setting the size of the quantum leap to be achieved; taking stock of the business and market opportunities; evaluating strategic options; and creating business development projects. Participants could be encouraged to think as futureologists and horizon scanners do.

Strategic workshops should be held away from company offices to avoid the distraction of day-to-day matters. A country-house hotel is a suitable venue.

Preferably, the participants will meet for dinner the evening before the workshop commences. This provides an opportunity for the chief executive to set the scene and ensures that a prompt start will be made in the morning. Two working days is probably the amount of time required to address the agenda of crucial issues for success.

Features which help to achieve a productive strategic workshop include:

- an agenda restricted to issues of strategic importance; lesser matters must be ruthlessly excluded
- precirculated and concise 'position papers' to provide the background to each item on the agenda
- skilled chairing to ensure that people say what they believe, while avoiding personal criticism
- a summary of agreement reached, decisions made and further action committed, circulated promptly after the workshop.

Strategic workshops:

- create belief in, and commitment to the achievement of the vision, with a clear sense of collective accountability
- improve teamwork and motivation
- are an effective management development method to help functional directors and executives to develop a broader outlook on the overall needs of the business.

It is important that the first strategic workshop a business holds is productive, because otherwise people are likely to be less enthusiastic on the next occasion.

Strategic workshops are deceptively complex, and previous experience is valuable. Consequently, some companies have used outside advice on the first occasion to ensure success. A typical role of an outside adviser would be to:

- interview each participant to identify the crucial issues for success that should be part of the agenda
- agree the agenda with the chief executive
- advise upon the format and content of the position papers
- participate during the workshop to ensure that the issues are addressed rigorously, and that positive decisions are taken and further action agreed.

Many large companies use strategic workshops in each separate subsidiary, as well as holding them at group level. Some companies go further, and use strategic workshops within major functions of subsidiary companies selectively. Strategic workshops have been widely used in professional partnerships, restricting attendance either to the management committee of the whole business or the relevant partners in a particular country or regional office.

Turnaround of a loss-making business

This is a testing ground for strategic thinkers because it is obviously essential to succeed in the short term in order to survive so that there will be a long term. It emphasises that it is no good concentrating on long-term strategy at the expense of real short-term strategic urgency.

An important way to achieve growth in profits is to turn round loss-making businesses. A surprising number of large companies have one or more subsidiaries making losses at any time. The number of private companies that fail is further proof of loss-making businesses. One response is a desire to sell the loss-making business, which is really an attempt to walk away from a situation which is both a problem and an opportunity. Even if a buyer is found, the purchase price is likely to be lower than net asset value. If a loss-making business is sold to the existing management, interesting questions are raised. What will they do different from before? Why was this not done at the direction of the group previously? The opportunity is to turn the business into profit before considering selling it, because even if a sale makes sense, it will be easier to achieve and a much higher price should be obtained.

Initial action

It must be recognised that the turnaround of a loss-making business is unlikely to happen unless a new chief executive is appointed. Yet some groups tolerate losses from the same subsidiary for years before appointing a new chief executive to turn it round. This is nothing less than costly and unacceptable procrastination. Strategic plans which are really a recipe for 'more of the same', without proposing drastic action, should be rejected. Equally, financial analysis alone will not produce the necessary results.

Almost certainly, the essential first step is to appoint a new chief executive of the subsidiary with the authority to take the action needed to turn losses into acceptable profits as quickly as possible.

If there is an immediate cash flow crisis threatening the survival of the business, then tackling this must be the main priority. Specific action which may be needed as a matter of urgency includes:

- meeting the bank and secured creditors to avoid receivership
- negotiating a delayed payment schedule for outstanding major trade creditors wherever possible, while reassuring people that effective corrective action is being taken quickly
- concentrating efforts on the collection of outstanding customer debts
- adopting a selective policy for paying creditors at least some of the money owed to them to ensure continuity of essential supplies and services and to avoid damaging legal action wherever possible.

Then there is a strong case for the newly appointed chief executive to make his or her presence felt. The seriousness of the situation should be brought home by a variety of measures such as:

- terminating the employment of all temporary staff until further notice
  - if this could damage the business, someone is likely to scream loudly enough
- requiring personal approval of all overseas travel
  - the purpose of the visit must justify the expense involved and wherever appropriate the proposed visit schedule should be reviewed before approval is given
- suspending non-essential expense until further notice
  - for example, the employment of contractors to redecorate offices, the replacement of company cars, and so on
- delaying all non-essential capital expenditure for a period
- making all recruitment, including the replacing of existing staff, subject to chief executive approval
- eliminating any lavish entertainment or visible extravagance.

The impact of these measures may be modest in relation to the seriousness of the problems which exist. Nonetheless, they will make the point that the decks are being cleared in readiness for tough action to be taken where appropriate.

Identifying the causes of losses

The next step is to identify the main causes of the loss. The chief executive needs to talk to each member of the board and other members of the management team. Surprisingly often, the main causes quickly become apparent to someone newly appointed to the company. Possible causes may be:

- overhead costs are excessive in relation to sales volume
- the production cost of the service or product is too high compared with the market price
- there is overcapacity in the industry sector because of falling demand
- the marketing and selling efforts are ineffective and too costly
- product performance and customer benefits are no longer competitive
- poor product quality and reliability have undermined sales
- expensive subcontract work is needed to compensate for internal shortcomings.

Urgent financial analysis should be carried out to confirm the main causes of the losses. Aspects which need to be assessed include:

- the marginal profit percentage produced by each product or service group
- major customer profitability
- the break-even point of the business based upon existing overhead levels
- the maximum affordable fixed overhead costs to break even on present sales volume and prices.

Time does not allow for precise financial analysis to be done. The need is for sufficiently accurate information to be produced quickly.

The newly appointed chief executive needs to avoid being overwhelmed by day-to-day problems. A dispassionate and detailed examination of the business must be the main priority. A good way to start is to spend some time with sales staff. Accompanying people on sales visits to clients and prospective clients is often revealing. The shortcomings of the company are likely to become transparent. Problems such as unsatisfactory product performance, uncompetitive prices, unacceptable quality and reliability, late delivery and ineffective selling will be quickly exposed.

Visits with sales staff will expose any shortcoming of the sales support team. So it makes sense to examine sales support departments next. Only then should attention be focused on marketing activities.

The contribution of marketing to the business needs to be measured. The level of expense needs to be assessed critically. It is all too easy for marketing activity to be confused with marketing effectiveness. In one company, the marketing staff was cut from 17 people to eight. Afterwards, it was generally accepted throughout the business that the contribution of marketing had increased substantially as a result of better direction, despite operating with a much smaller staff.

The production and delivery of the products or services supplied to customers should be the next point to come under scrutiny. Questions which need to be answered include:

- What scope is there to apply value-engineering techniques to the specification of products or services?
- What is the speed of delivery and the reliability of delivery promises?
- How much business is lost by late or part delivery?
- What bottlenecks exist and how can these be overcome?
- What needs to be done to improve product or service quality and reliability?
- What can be done to reduce costs significantly?
- What buy versus make opportunities should be evaluated?
- What additional expenditure would produce an attractive financial return quickly?

The role and contribution of head office needs critical examination. The minimum possible number of staff needed should be determined. Wherever the cost implications are acceptable, operating businesses should be responsible for providing the full range of services needed so they can be managed as autonomous units.

Administration costs should be attacked. Satisfactory answers are needed to questions such as:

- What would happen if the work was left undone?
- Why is it done so often?
- Why is it done in such an expensive way?
- If it really needs to be done, how could it be handled at much lower cost or outsourced?

Research and development can prove a difficult area to tackle. The chief executive appointed may lack technical knowledge compared with senior development staff. This need not necessarily be a disadvantage.

Questions to be answered which cut through the technical complexities include:

- How does the level of research and development expenditure compare with that of leading competitors?
- What percentage of total research and development costs is spent on:
  - pure research?
  - new product development?
  - further development of existing, and possibly tired, products?
- What percentage of current sales is represented by new products or services introduced during the last five years?
- What is the percentage of sales from new products and services contributed by:
  - internal research and development
  - licensing, royalty or distribution agreements
  - joint venture co-operation?
- How are research and development projects evaluated commercially and financially before work is commenced?
- Is there adequate liaison between research and development, marketing and production staff?
- Are effective project-management and cost-control techniques used?
- Which projects have proved to be expensive failures, and what lessons have been learned?
- What new projects should be authorised or evaluated to meet the market needs?

Rationalising the business

Now it is necessary to address the need for rationalisation of the business and a reduction in staff levels and overhead costs in order to achieve a break-even situation quickly. The range of products and services offered may need drastic pruning. A list of products and services in descending order of the amount of either marginal profit or gross profit produced by each one may be revealing. In one company, out of nearly 500 products, six accounted for more than 80 per cent of the total marginal profit produced. Substantial reduction of the product range was achieved without any significant adverse customer reaction.

Staff will have realised that redundancies will happen, without having been told. The sooner the redundancies are announced, the sooner the uncertainty is ended. In the meantime, the staff most likely to leave are the more talented people, who will find it easier to get other jobs – this is another reason for speed.

The first decision is the overall number of people to be made redundant to achieve the cost reduction required, compatible with maintaining a viable infrastructure within the business and leaving an affordable level of overhead costs. Any suggestion of rateable cuts in each department must be rejected. The chief executive should agree with the manager of each department the number of redundancies and total cost reduction required. Disproportionately large cuts may be required at head office and in administration departments, and some modest recruitment may even be necessary at the sharp end of the business, such as direct sales staff or installation engineers.

Each manager should be required to propose a schedule showing the required redundancies and cost reduction. The chief executive should review each list and be satisfied that an objective selection has been made. Then people need to be informed. This should be done face to face and handled with understanding, generosity and compassion. Trade unions will need to be notified where appropriate. If possible, people should be given help to obtain other jobs. There is no ideal time to announce redundancies, but a Friday afternoon makes sense. This means that only those people still employed by the company will return to work on the following Monday morning. Disaffected people who have been made redundant must not be allowed to linger.

It is important that all of the redundancies are announced at once. Morale will be affected, but it will be much worse if people are left to speculate when the next round of redundancies will be announced. The sooner that the business needs to start recruiting people again, the better it is for morale.

At this stage, the reduced level of fixed costs will be known by the chief executive and the overall percentage marginal profit will soon be achieved. So it is easy to calculate the annual sales value required to break even. This should be translated into a monthly sales target needed to break even, and the management team should collectively be committed to the goal of the first month in which the break-even sales value will be exceeded and so eliminate the losses.

The next step should be to involve the board or executive committee in setting revised and demanding sales and profit forecasts for the remainder of the current year. The opportunity should be taken to improve monthly management information in order to provide people with the information needed to manage the business effectively.

Rigorous budget preparation is needed for the next financial year. People must realise that the elimination of losses is not enough; it is only the first and relatively easy stage on the road to financial recovery. The goal must be to achieve an acceptable return on the operating assets employed as quickly as possible.

In a turnaround situation, an important part of the budget should be a number of profit-improvement projects. Each one should:

- be designed to achieve rapid profit and cash flow improvement

- have a member of the board accountable for timely and successful completion.

Once the initial surgery has been carried out and profit-improvement projects initiated, it is time to get down to business development in earnest. A fundamental issue needs to be addressed. Now that initial turnaround work has been done, should the chief executive continue in post or be replaced by someone better suited to carry out the business development work? This may seem a surprising question to raise. It may well be, however, that the turnaround person is not ideally suited to stay on through the medium term to achieve the business development needed.

The evidence available shows that surgery and short-term profit-improvement action are likely to eliminate losses but that major new initiatives are needed to achieve an acceptable financial return.

There is no substitute for:

- creating a vision statement

- adopting the quantum leap approach

- identifying and evaluating strategic options

- establishing an effective organisation structure

- setting up major business development projects.

15 Business plans

This chapter is not about putting forward ideas, proposals, and so on for approval, but about preparing a formal, written business plan. It is complementary to Chapter 14.

Introduction

Preparing and presenting business plans is an important and time-consuming part of any senior manager's business life. A business plan must be written as a sales document, because the purpose is usually either to obtain board approval or to raise external finance (from a bank or venture capital house, for example). Equally, the face-to-face presentation meeting must be treated as a sales meeting. The written words are important, but the passion, belief and commitment conveyed in a presentation meeting are of the essence.

The focus of the business plan should be to:

- set realistic and achievable financial goals for sales, profit and cash flow

- outline the commercial rationale, performance and quality standards required

- identify the human resources, capital expenditure and working capital needed

- recognise the key business risks and how these will be managed.

Performance against business plans needs to be measurable and should be monitored regularly. It is not enough that the financial goals are being met, because this might be as a result of deferring business development projects and capital expenditure, which will undermine subsequent performance. All-round financial, development and commercial progress must be measured against the plan.

Business plans need regular appraisal, updating and amending, ideally six monthly and at least annually. If a major external event occurs such as the 11 September terrorist attacks, the Iraq war or the domino spread of disturbances in Arab states and earthquakes in Japan, significant changes may be needed. Remember the armed forces adage about war plans, which are prepared exhaustively in modern warfare: no plan ever survives first contact with the enemy. In other words, planning is essential but plans need to be adapted to changing circumstances.

The timescale of business plans is important. Most people nowadays choose a three-year period, because the business world and technology are changing so rapidly and often in unpredictable ways, whereas a decade ago, five-year plans were commonplace. It must be recognised, however, that many three-year plans will need to include projects which will take much longer to come to fruition, such as a major development project to create a new drug for diabetes or the next generation of mobile phones incorporating full feature computing, internet and video capabilities.

This chapter focuses on internal business plans – Chapter 16 outlines the main differences required in writing a plan to obtain external finance.

Key ingredients of internal business plans

This section outlines a proven framework for an internal business plan, which can be adapted to suit your particular circumstances.

A typical contents page with page numbering (and there should always be one) of an internal business plan should include:

1   executive summary

2   performance against and key changes to previous plan

3   main products and/or services

4   market analysis and marketing plans

5   manufacturing and operations

6   information technology

7   organisation structure and human resources

8   risk analysis and management

9   business development projects and progress milestones

10 financial projections

11 appendices.

Too many business plans are far too long. Ideally, the executive summary should be a single page and should never exceed two pages. The main narrative should be a maximum of 15 pages. Financial projections require only three pages. The appendices should be presented and bound separately, but a contents page and page numbering are essential to allow the reader to quickly locate any back-up information of interest.

Executive summary

This should give the reader a snapshot of the significant contents of the plan, including a summary of sales, profit and cash flow.

Performance against and key changes to previous plan

Most companies require the annual preparation and presentation of three-year business plans, so the previous plan still has two years remaining. Yet few companies demand that this section is included, despite the fact that many people do not refer to their previous plan before rewriting it. The financial and commercial performance in the first year of the previous plan, together with significant changes for the future, lend credibility to the latest plan or grounds for justifiable scepticism.

Main products and/or services

This should describe the main products and/or services, their competitive advantage in the market and how future developments will yield even greater success. Any technological, intellectual property, regulatory and R&D advantages should be defined.

Depending on the nature of the products and/or services, it may be useful to provide details on such aspects as the development cycle of new products/services; what new products/services are planned to follow on from those offered at the start; the level of protection (patent, trade mark or copyright) for each product/service.

Market analyses and marketing plans

This section is crucial because it is the foundation for the whole plan. It should present quantitative information about the current market; anticipated future demand and trends; and anticipated initiatives by both existing and new competitors. The marketing plan should outline the principal actions needed to achieve the market share, sales and selling prices included in the business plan. So how should this part of the plan be tackled? It is recommended that you break it down into four parts.

The industry/sector

The industry/sector that you are in needs to be defined in terms of:

- its main characteristics, by region or country as appropriate

- its main customers

- the applications for your products/services

- the likely trends and

- the outlook (changes in size, and so on) over the next three years.

The market

Market analysis requires precision. An overall assessment of the market may well conceal important opportunities and threats. Each market segment must be identified and assessed. For example, a corporate finance boutique operates in the merger market generally, but it needs to assess individual segments such as the sale of private companies, groups selling subsidiaries, management buy-outs and buy-ins, taking public companies private, and so on. Customer success factors in each segment need to be targeted:

- What are the critical elements (reliability, quality, price, service, and so on)?

- What is the customer profile (size of company, identity of decision-maker, number of customers)?

- What are the buying habits (size of orders, competitive tendering, supplier approval, changeability) seasonal variations?

- What success has already been achieved with customers or what interest has been shown to date?

The competition

Due weight must be given to an appraisal of current and likely future competitors, with theirs and your strengths and weaknesses objectively assessed.

- Who are the competitors now (and who are they likely to be in the future)?

- How do you compare?

- How will they respond?

- Why will you succeed?

The marketing activities

These need to be separated into marketing and sales.

Marketing: Your plans for positioning the products/services in terms of quality, price, service, and so on should be set out and details given of plans for:

- distribution
- promotion, advertising and use of the web and social networking
- pricing (demand or cost-based, discounts, planned levels for the future?)
- customer service and support
- geographical penetration (domestic, international)
- prioritising opportunities.

Sales: You need to show how sales will be achieved, analysing multi-channel selling opportunities (online, through retail outlets, agents, franchises, a sales-force?) and how prospective customers will be identified and converted into actual customers. The plan for operating through agents and so on needs to be set out showing terms, conditions and predictions. For operating a salesforce, the detail should include size and geographical coverage, productivity (calls and conversion rates, average size of each sale, repeat order pattern) and remuneration systems (basic and commission levels).

For websites, search-engine optimisation, clicks, conversions, order, size, returns and so on will need collating electronically.

For retail outlets, site size, sales staff, sales per square foot, and so on will need to be cited with back-up evidence.

You may think that this section is too detailed, but you would be wrong. Some managers base their sales projections for the next three years on an overall percentage growth each year, which is inadequate. Rigorous analysis is essential to provide a solid foundation for any business plan.

Manufacturing and operations

This section should explain how production will be accomplished or how customer services will be carried out, identifying:

- suppliers (both internal and external) and what are the likely developments
- key production/operating advantages
- present facilities, capacity and future plans
- critical aspects (parts, machinery, outsourcing etc.)

- costs of production (and impact of volume on them)
- human resources required.

Information technology (IT)

IT, or ICT (Information and Communications Technology), capability is of such fundamental importance today and in the foreseeable future that it merits separate consideration and treatment. E-commerce is so important that some sectors, e.g. airlines, impose a significant surcharge or even do not allow telephone reservations. In many markets, rules of business which were dominant only five years ago are being swept away.

A business simply cannot afford to pursue a continuous and gradual improvement in IT capability (which now includes the internet/web), because future success, or even survival, may be at risk. The foundation for an effective IT strategy is awareness. The analysis required includes:

- how the major companies in your sector are using IT to increase sales, provide better customer service and reduce operating costs
- the wider technological developments which could provide opportunities for your company (such as direct voice input for data processing or the increased use of social networking sites).
- how your direct competitors are using IT to gain an edge.

Serendipity is inadequate. Someone needs to have a voracious appetite to collate and analyse information as a prelude to formulating a robust IT plan.

Organisation structure and human resources

An organisation chart, with staff numbers by department, provides a useful overview. Senior manager recruitment, human resources development and staff incentive initiatives should be outlined.

Risk analysis and management

Significant risks should be identified and contingency plans outlined. It must be recognised that effective risk management requires that all significant risks are identified, regardless of how improbable they appear, because the consequences could be damaging if something happens.

For example, a facilities management company may have a client which accounts for 30 per cent of turnover and more than 33 per cent of total gross profit, whereas the second largest contract represents only 5 per cent of turnover. Furthermore, the contract has just been renewed for another five-year term and their chief executive is delighted with the service.

The risk is that the contract allows the customer to give six months' notice of premature termination, but it seems highly improbable. If the customer is acquired, however, the enlarged group may decide to reduce the number of suppliers. The message is clear: if the risk is significant, it must be addressed even though the probability seems remote.

Business development projects and progress milestones

These are described in Chapter 14 and should be summarised in the business plan.

Financial projections

Financial information must be presented in an accessible way in the plan, because the supporting details should be included in the appendices.

A separate page is required for:

- the profit and loss account
- cash flow, including external financing required
- the balance sheet.

Each page should list:

- previous two years' actual figures to give perspective
- latest current year forecast
- next three years' projections
- key assumptions used (for example, the number of debtor days each year).

Appendices

The appendices are likely to include supporting data on:

- projected sales (by key customer, product or service, country, anticipated price increases, and so on)
- a list of major capital expenditure projects, with the attendant working capital and overhead cost implications
- principal research and development projects to be implemented

- marketing plan
- freehold and leasehold premises to be acquired or disposed of.

There can be no recommended list for the appendices because the aim is to provide back-up information to support key aspects of the plan and to convince the reader of the rigour and analysis underpinning it.

16 Acquisitions and disposals of unquoted companies

This chapter deals with the acquisitions and disposals of unquoted companies and not with the takeover of a 'public' company. It is written in summary, checklist style to point up the key areas for attention to indicate possible pitfalls. The structure of the chapter is as follows:

* buying

* selling

* negotiating

* managing post-completion.

As in every deal there will be a buyer and a seller, the whole section is relevant to each player in the acquisition/disposal process. Note that the checklist approach taken precludes examination of detailed aspects, including the tax and legal issues.

An analysis of various acquisition deals (which had worked and which had not) concluded that the keys to a good deal are:

* have a strategic purpose

* know the sector and country

* investigate the business thoroughly

* make realistic future projections and assumptions

* integrate carefully and fast

* don't pay too much

* don't borrow too much to finance the deal.

Buying

How to plan for successful acquisitions

Select attractive market segments and countries

- based on assessment of:
    - future market demand and capacity
    - anticipated impact of technology
    - existing and likely competitors
    - ease of entry by acquisition or start-up.
- wherever attractive, pursue opportunities for:
    - market leadership
    - increased market share
    - dominance of a niche market.

Define commercial rationale for acquiring the target

- analyse sound reasons (as well as selecting market segments), for example:
    - extending product range
    - acquiring key sales outlets
    - protecting a source of supply
    - the minimum profits required
    - the shape of the organisation into which it will fit
    - the desired location(s)
    - the key features for success.

How to find attractive sellers

Use the knowledge within the business

- brainstorm
- brief buyers, salespeople, technical staff
- identify what else your customers buy
- visit your sales outlets and see what else they sell.

Desk research prospective targets

- various commercial sector surveys

- electronic databases
- trade association membership lists
- trade exhibitions and press features for the sector
- internet.

Put bread on the water
- include a paragraph in annual report
- get editorial coverage in trade press and online
- when press releasing an acquisition – say 'more wanted'.

Involve intermediaries and advisers
- notify intermediaries and professional advisers
    - major accountants – disposal register (cost about 1.5 per cent)
    - business brokers (cost on reducing scale: 5 to 1 per cent based on deal value)
    - merchant banks and corporate finance boutiques
    - venture capital funds seeking a sale.
- consider outside help for acquisition search
    - agree acquisition profile
    - demand exclusivity.
- beware of buying what is for sale instead of what you want to buy.

Consider alternatives to acquisition

Start-up
- internal resources needed
- external funding needed
- viability of a start-up plan in terms of time needed to build a robust business.

Distribution of manufacturing rights
- as a way of getting to know target
- as an alternative to acquisition.

Minority equity stake
- to lead to eventual acquisition with a formula for control or purchase
- to obtain a non-executive directorship for influence.

Joint venture or consortium

- pick compatible partners

- anticipate corporate culture problems

- establish management accountability

- identify exit routes, because the original rationale often expires within a few years.

Majority equity control

- may be useful overseas.

Earn-out deals

- relevant for many private companies

- beware of pitfalls (see later).

Agree an acquisition profile

Write it down

- to focus the search

- to pre-sell internally

- to avoid abortive effort

- to brief intermediaries.

Write an acquisition profile giving

- the nature of the business, the products/services required

- the maximum price affordable

- the nature of the consideration (for example, cash, shares, loan stock, and so on).

Consider using outside help

- shortlist targets (accounts and product/service literature)

- list rejected companies (and state key reason)

- adviser to telephone key person to explore sale

- agree completion date and a fixed fee for the search work

- legal completion fee (about 1.5 per cent)

- don't pay retainers to receive occasional acquisition opportunities.

Advertise selectively and effectively

- the *Financial Times* and *Wall Street Journal*, for example, reach owners and intermediaries
- trade press – less expensive
- avoid box number – puts people off
- specify market sector, profit and location – give company name, contact person and telephone number.

How to handle the initial approach to a target company

- telephone preferred to writing
- private company (find out key shareholder or institutional investors)
- subsidiary (approach the group)
- use an approach by a third party
    - to protect identity initially
    - to 'sell' a possibly unwelcome acquirer
    - to save management time
    - to benefit from their expertise.

How to approach the investigation needed before negotiation proceeds

- confirm your wish to buy
- identify skeletons and hidden gold, for example:
    - tax irregularities
    - recent loss of major customers
    - overseas opportunities unexploited
    - cost rationalisation opportunities
    - surplus assets and working capital
- project future profits and cash flows
- focus due diligence investigation if deal agreed.

How to carry out a comprehensive assessment of the target

Check out:

- sales history and projections (and identify one-offs)
- key customers, suppliers, contracts and renewal dates
- pricing (opportunity to increase or need to hold?)
- order book (is it an 'asset' or a 'liability'?)
- sales and distribution channels
- competitors
- IT capability and compatibility
- production capacity and efficiency
- leases and property issues, including cost of refurbishment
- capital investment needed for expansion
- accounting policies and provisions
- R&D projects
- key people
- salaries, bonuses, fringe benefits
- share option schemes
- pension fund
  - final salary scheme
  - over or under funded?
  - money purchase scheme
  - insured or invested?
- health and safety issues
- contingent liabilities, for example
  - litigation threat
  - warranty claims
  - environmental pollution time bomb
- compatibility of corporate culture and style
- owner extravagances
  - spouses and/or relatives employed
  - planes, boats, houses
  - entertainment and sponsorship.

How to use investigating accountants effectively

- meet the team leader
- agree written terms of reference
- insist on a budgetary fee limit
- agree number of people and timetable
- start only after heads of agreement signed
- set date for receipt of report
- ask for verbal debrief as well.

(It is not essential to use your auditing firm.)

How to handle overseas acquisitions

Select the country by assessing

- political stability
  - civil unrest
  - national strikes
  - local wars.
- cultural and social background
  - discrimination against foreign ownership
  - language skills
  - education standards
  - employee relations
  - communications and services
  - acceptance of expatriates
  - expatriates' safety.
- legal requirements
  - equity ownership restrictions
  - government agency approval needed
  - monopoly and antitrust considerations
  - exchange control
  - employment law
  - reporting requirements.

- taxation and repatriation of funds
  - taxation rate
  - incentives and tariffs
  - withholding taxes
  - double taxation agreements
  - repatriation of profits and capital.

Within the chosen country

- stick to market segments/business you know
- check sufficient acquisition candidates exist
- investigate likely purchase prices
- consider the merit of local equity partner as a minority investor
- learn from its banks in the UK
- choice of advisers?
  - overseas bank (contact UK branch first)
  - management consultants
  - auditors (overseas branches)
  - local lawyers.
- acquisition search
  - known targets
  - search based in the country.

Selling

How to plan a successful sale

Consider the alternatives to selling

- management buy-out or buy-in
- sell equity stake to financial institution
- merge, using 'paper' (that is, shares not cash)
- acquire (with institutional backing)
- buy in some of own shares
- obtain a stockmarket listing.

Decide when to sell

- show current year progress and future growth
- avoid a recent setback or current year forecast loss
- people often hold on too long
- beware of serious illness
- realise temporary scarcity value
- approaching financial year end is a good time.

Decide what to sell

- include related businesses, for example
  - overseas subsidiaries
  - another business which conflicts
- shares or assets and business
- property to be included or excluded.

Preparation needed to get the best price

- ensure share structure is simple
- avoid shares held by children under 18
- corporation tax, VAT and PAYE (in order and up to date?)
- ensure a tax investigation is not pending or in progress
- capital gains tax planning
- budgets, monthly accounts and year-end forecasts give confidence
- assess freehold and leasehold value
- employment contracts in order
- pension fund (especially transfer from a group)
- intellectual property (transfer ownership or give licence)
- acceptable staff incentive schemes
- no major litigation in progress or pending such as a patent dispute on a key product
- share option scheme implications.

How to find attractive buyers

Use the knowledge within the business

- always record unsolicited approaches
- identify companies:
  - offering related products/services
  - with a product/service gap
  - with a similar business in other countries
- direct competitors may be less attractive purchasers.

Involve a professional adviser

- business brokers
  - no deal/no fee basis
  - unlikely to provide professional advice
  - beware of gossip factor
- major and medium-sized accounting firms
  - challenge joining disposal register
  - will provide comprehensive professional advice
- corporate finance boutiques
  - will provide comprehensive professional advice
  - may specialise in smaller deals.

Consider advertising

- may produce unexpected purchasers
- don't reveal identity unintentionally
- FT reaches buyers and intermediaries
- ask for written responses via a Box No
- may produce 40 to 125 replies (buyers, advisers, individuals)
- eliminate unwanted replies
- get confidentiality agreement signed
- then send written synopsis.

Use a controlled auction, if appropriate

- consider controlled auction
  - when firmly committed to sell

- when confident acceptable offer obtainable
  - prepare detailed sales memorandum
  - announce by press release or advert
  - popular to sell larger subsidiaries, but rarely appropriate for private companies
- handle a controlled auction
  - get confidentiality agreement signed
  - send out sales memorandum
  - set date for outline offers
  - shortlist buyers to meet management
  - seller may give standard contract
  - invite confirmed/revised offers
  - negotiate with preferred purchaser.

How to handle approaches

From an intermediary

- check them out
- find out company and individual represented.

From a prospective purchaser

- if interested, meet on neutral ground
- establish authority of individual
- may provide market knowledge or mutual business opportunity
- be guarded
- take professional advice at outset
- consider seeking other purchasers.

Agree, before providing further information

- ball-park price or valuation basis
- scope of information to be provided
  - probably meet two or three people off-site for about a half a day
- information not to be provided until heads of agreement signed, for example
  - customer analysis
  - research know-how

Negotiating

How to value the business

Buyers

- should base their valuation on:
  - their projections of profits and cash flows
  - any upstream or downstream benefits.
- should assess
  - balance sheet worth and surplus assets
  - cost/time of alternatives to acquisitions.

Sellers

- should assess:
  - value from the buyer's standpoint
  - other buyer or options
  - effect on their lifestyle and retirement
  - if a sale now is premature
  - strategic significance or rarity value.

Calculation of adjusted profits for most recent year

- buyers should adjust profit before tax for changes that will be made
  - different accounting policies, for example, depreciation
  - need to appoint finance director
  - higher insurance cover needed
  - wage and salary differentials
  - additional pension costs.
- sellers will point out:
  - excessive directors' salaries and pensions
  - cost of relatives no longer employed
  - boats and planes
  - allocated management changes
  - significant one-off events, such as a large bad debt or revenue costs of US launch or relocation costs.

Calculation of adjusted profits and cash flows for current and future years should identify

- assumptions used in forecasts

- what the buyer can add, for example:
    - additional sales opportunities
    - cost rationalisation and reduction
    - tighter financial control
    - upstream or downstream benefits.

How to assess the value of the business

Price earnings ratio (widely used, but ignores cash flow)

- attempts to calculate 'market value' of a stockmarket listed company

- provides useful benchmark for sellers

- PE ratio = $\dfrac{\text{Current share price}}{\text{Earnings per share for previous year}}$

- empirical evidence shows unquoted companies often sell at a discount to listed company PE ratios
    - discount is typically 33-40 per cent and up to 50 per cent if the whole sector is hard-pressed, unless strategic significance or rarity value exists (when a premium PE ratio may be obtained).

Return on investment (gives short-/medium-term indicator)

- ROI = $\dfrac{\text{Profit before tax}}{\text{Net investment}}$

- Net investment = Purchase price plus further cash investment needed, minus surplus assets realised

- Many listed companies making acquisitions seek at least 20 per cent ROI in second full financial year after acquisition.

Discounted cash flow (Chapter 11 addresses key issues of cash flow)
in acquisitions deals

- Initial investment = Initial purchase price

- Annual cash flow = Cash generated/needed for operations plus surplus assets realised minus earn-out payments

- use percentage of internal rate of return and discounted pay-back period methods

- use sensitivity analysis of 'what if?' questions.

Net asset backing (relevant for loss makers)

- seek to buy at a discount to net assets because:
    - relieves owners of a problem
    - acquirer may need a safety margin.

Take into account

- impact on earnings per share (important for listed companies)
    - calculate impact of current year's earnings per share
    - check when dilution eliminates
    - take into account earn-out payments
- rarity or scarcity value (premium others may be prepared to pay).

Worked example of valuation (for non-accountants)

	£'000
Previous year profit before tax of seller	725
Effect of buyer's depreciation policy	35
Allow for extra cost of:	
Financial director	(75)
Wage and salary differentials	(25)
Higher insurance cover	(10)
Add back:	
Excess cost of directors' salaries and personal pensions	100
Relatives no longer required	40
Annual cost of company boat	60
Adjusted profit before tax	850

Figures in £'000	Last year	This year	Next year	Year after
Adjusted profit before tax	850	930	1,050	1,200
Assume 30 per cent corporation tax in UK	(255)	(280)	(315)	(360)
Profit after tax	595	650	735	840

Assume the sector average PE ratio = 18.0 (published in *Financial Times*)
Assume a discount of 40 percent = 7.0
Earnings multiple to be paid = 11.0

Likely purchase price = 11.0 × £595,000 = about £6.6m

If buyer wanted 20 per cent pre-tax ROI in year after next:

Likely purchase price = £1.2m divided by 20 per cent

= about £6m

These methods give only a rough idea of likely value but may be helpful for a non-accountant.

How to approach an earn-out deal

Basis of an earn-out deal

- buy 100 per cent of equity now
- pay some purchase consideration initially
  - to reflect reasonable price for profits to date
  - not less than net asset backing
- additional payment for increased future profits before tax
- sellers should think carefully about earn-out periods longer than the next two years, too much uncertainty
- buyers should put a cap or maximum limit on earn-out payments.

An earn-out deal makes sense if:

- business success still depends on owners
- asset backing low (for example, service company)
- profits forecast to increase rapidly
- profits at risk (for example, loss of a major customer by failure to renew a contract)
- an owner is to continue as MD.

Earn-out issues to be addressed by the seller include:

- definition of profit before tax for earn-out and contract needs to specify:
  - accounting policies
  - management charges (for example, payroll and legal, and so on)
  - cost of central services used (for example, distribution)
  - intra-group pricing policies
  - cost of finance to be provided
  - dividend policy.

- management control:
    - need to agree before structuring deal:
        - changes which will alter costs (such as appointment of financial director) business opportunities to be pursued (such as start-up in US next year)
        - no-go areas (for example, competing against other subsidiaries)
    - need to establish at the outset:
        - board control
        - preparation of budgets, monthly accounts and year end forecasts, sensitive issues (e.g. initiating litigation or dealing with the media)

(Note to buyers: if business starts to fall apart – move in!)

Worked example of earn-out deal (for non-accountants)

- Consider a company organising conferences and incentive events for major car manufacturers in Europe, the US and East Asia. Future growth depends on the companies' further expansion in the automotive sector, but primarily on gaining major clients in the lucrative pharmaceuticals sector. The net asset backing is only £900. Profit growth will be small next year as a result of recruiting a dedicated team for the pharmaceuticals industry.

Figures in £'000	Last year	This year	Next year	Year after
Adjusted profit before tax	1,500	2,000	2,100	3,000
Assume 30 per cent corporation tax	(450)	(600)	(630)	(900)
Adjusted profit after tax	1,050	1,400	1,470	2,100

The deal agreed was:

- £11.0m on legal completion
- plus £0.5m for achieving £2m pre-tax profit this year
- plus five times pre-tax profits in excess of £2m next year
- and the year after, up to a maximum total deal value of £18m

Initial PE ratio $= \dfrac{£11.0m}{£1.05m} = 10.5$

Final PE ratio $= \dfrac{£17.0m}{£2.1m} = 8.1$ for on target profit performance in each year

ROI year

after next $= \dfrac{£3.0m}{£17.0m}$ = 17.6 per cent

How to negotiate the deal

Skills required

- previous experience
- negotiation expertise
- tax and legal knowledge.

Helpful elements

- keep team as small as possible
- set a negotiation price limit at outset
- identify any deal-breaker issues.

Deal format stage of negotiation, discuss and agree

- share purchase versus assets and business
- outright purchase versus earn-out deal
- assets to be excluded
- directors and relatives to retire/resign
- attractive forms of purchase consideration
- conditional purchase contract (to defer capital gains tax a year)
- date for final negotiation.

Possible forms of purchase consideration

- cash
- shares
- loan stock or loan notes
- pre-completion dividend
- personal pension contributions
- purchase of assets
- service contracts
- consultancy agreements.

Typical agenda for final negotiation

- update since last meeting
- confirmation of what is included in the deal
- purchase by directors of assets (for example, cars/boats)
- contracts for directors/key staff
- treatment of existing share options
- transfer of pension fund
- intellectual property
- earn-out formula and period
- key warranties and indemnities
- purchase price and consideration
- timetable to legal completion.

Timetable of dates to legal completion

- signing of heads of agreements or letter of intent including:
  - period of exclusivity
  - non disclosure
  - any cost indemnity for vendors
- receipt of share purchase agreement
- start and duration of accounting investigation
- receipt by buyer of accountant's report
- date reserved for principals and lawyers to finalise contract
- receipt of disclosure statement
- venue for signing contract at legal completion.

Managing post-completion

Prepare for first day

- first impressions count
- listen to advice from vendors
- involve continuing directors in announcement
- plan to tell customers and suppliers

- notify trade unions as appropriate
- prepare and plan for day one.

Handle first day successfully

- meet management, staff and unions
- consider a meeting for announcements, for example with corporate videos and questions
- prepare for anticipated questions
- avoid rash assurances
- demonstrate a real interest and concern
- recognise rumours and anxiety abound
- tell your own staff who may be affected.

Achieve financial control immediately (concentrate on essentials)

- capital investment and special revenue expense authorisation
- cash management
- head count and expense control
- reliable sales and profit forecasting.

Introduce uniform budgeting and reporting carefully

- immediate reporting changes may cause accounting chaos
- key requirement is reliable profit and cash figures for rest of year
- introduce uniform budgeting and reporting for new financial year
- need to train accountants and sell benefits to managers.

Manage and integrate the business effectively

- consider non-executive person to:
  - lead board meetings
  - help pursue opportunities with rest of group
  - restrict unnecessary visits by group staff
- identify special skills of owners

- have a plan to eliminate vulnerability (for example, major customer contract, technical expertise, and so on) and make sure it is completed before end of earn-out

- recognise dangers of forcing culture change on successful company

- assess the existing management talent

- consider injecting an MD designate, with a 'real' job

- arrange staff exchanges and visits

- visit major consumers, suppliers and overseas operations at board level

- learn from the acquisition

- for a loss-maker, appoint a full-time MD immediately.

17 Management buy-outs and buy-ins

To accumulate significant capital, any senior executive should seek an equity interest in addition to an attractive salary and bonus package.

Share options are widely given by quoted companies, but only a handful of top executives are likely to realise a serious amount of money in each company. Private companies may offer an equity stake or share options, but these often can be realised only when the company is sold or floated on a stock exchange.

For many senior executives in the UK, continental Europe or North America, however, a successful management buy-out (MBO) or management buy-in (MBI) can make them millionaires within five years.

Characteristics of an MBO or MBI

The members of the management team normally:

- invest some of their own money, often borrowed against the equity in their homes
- obtain a significant equity stake in the company, disproportionately much higher than their personal investment of cash
- can increase their equity stake by achieving exit valuation targets, often referred to as a 'ratchet mechanism'
- have executive management control of the business, although the financial institutions usually appoint one or more non-executive directors to represent their interest

Management buy-ins have become commonplace. An MBI requires executives with a proven track record in a closely related market sector. The driving force behind the growth in buy-ins has been the large amount of funds available and a shortage of buy-out opportunities with a strong management team in place. This has developed inevitably into BIMBO (Buy-in Management Buy-out) deals using a combination of existing managers in a business, strengthened by the injection of one or more managers from outside. Some successful buy-in teams have consisted of only two people, usually a chief executive and a marketing or finance director. The first step is to find a suitable target company which can be purchased.

Management buy-outs and buy-ins offer attractive opportunities to managers for the following reasons:

- Financial institutions typically want to realise their investments within three to five years, by selling the company or obtaining a stockmarket quotation. If an attractive opportunity to realise the investment arises much earlier, usually they will want to take it unless the management can convince them of the extra benefit from retaining the investment longer.

- The record of success has been very high, but of course there have been disappointments and failures.

- Managers have multiplied their original investment tens of times in the most successful cases.

Buy-outs and buy-ins really do offer the opportunity to create substantial personal capital within five years.

The initiative for a management buy-in must come from the managers themselves, and many buy-outs also arise from the initiative of the management team. Groups are prepared to consider divestment, including management buy-outs, for various reasons:

- The business is an unwanted part of a larger acquisition.

- It may no longer fit into the present commercial rationale for the group.

- The business may be too small to carry the overhead costs associated with a separate profit centre of a large group.

- The market is simply too competitive to carry the full weight of corporate overhead.

- The need to generate more cash or the wish to invest the proceeds in other opportunities.

Opportunities for management buy-outs, and possible buy-ins as well, include:

- privatisation of state-owned corporations

- taking a stockmarket-listed company private

- an alternative to an unwelcome bid for a listed company

- the purchase of a company in receivership

- owners of private companies wishing to retire or exit.

Suitable companies for an MBO or MBI

Despite the availability of opportunities, and the substantial potential rewards, common sense demands that a hard-headed and objective approach is adopted by the management team.

The essential ingredients for a suitable company are:

- a positive cash flow
- adequate asset backing
- right type of business
- good management team.

Each aspect will now be considered in turn below.

- Cash flow
    - cash is vital
    - cash generation is more important than profit in first 12–18 months
    - deals are financed largely by debt finance and overdraft, so some early repayment is needed.
- Asset backing
    - substantial net asset backing provides some security for debt finance
    - in a service company with little asset backing, demonstrable and consistent cash generation is key.
- Type of business
    - must have a long-term future to achieve an exit
    - current profitability or even losses are less important, provided that deliverable opportunities exist for increasing both profit and cash flow.
- Management team
    - each member of top management team must be prepared to invest, typically about six months salary
    - a proven chief executive or a director with the experience and credentials is essential
    - a financial director with hands-on cash management expertise is essential
    - the whole team need to be hungry to make serious money, not just seeking the comfort of keeping their existing jobs.

Making the approach

MBOs and MBIs need a somewhat different approach.

- MBOs
  - The company may be upset at the suggestion of a management buy-out and even tempted to replace the team leader if the business is not performing well. There is no point in taking the risk unless there is a determination to proceed.

  - One way to avoid this risk is for a specialist adviser to enquire whether or not a group is prepared to sell a business, without disclosing the identity of the bidder. This kind of approach is made frequently on behalf of corporate acquirers and has become increasingly common for management buy-outs. It is reasonable to expect the external adviser to charge for the initial approach.

- MBIs
  - When an approach is made to a target company, the prospective vendors will want an assurance that sufficient funds are available before exploring a possible sale of their business. It is important for the management buy-in team to make contact with prospective investors before contacting a target company. They will then be more convincing to a prospective vendor and able to complete the deal more quickly. Furthermore, some buy-in investors and corporate finance advisers know of companies which would be amenable to an approach, provided that a suitable management team is available.

Appoint a corporate finance adviser

The management team need a corporate finance adviser, usually a large accountancy firm, investment bank or corporate finance boutique, to:

- negotiate the purchase of the business from their present employers, knowing that if a deal does not take place they will wish to remain as employees

- select suitable institutional investors from the large number available

- present the management team, and their business plan, convincingly to prospective investors

- negotiate the best possible equity deal and ratchet mechanism for the management team with the institutional investor.

The benefits delivered for the management team by their corporate finance adviser should include:

- making an anonymous initial approach to the parent company
- providing the valuation and corporation tax expertise needed
- taking a tough negotiating stance with the parent company when necessary
- choosing the three or four most relevant buy-out investors, from the dozens which exist, for the management team to meet and to make their personal choice of financial partner
- having enough experience to know how attractive a deal it is possible to negotiate with the investors on behalf of the management team
- recommending a partner in a law firm with relevant experience.

Business plan

The purpose of the business plan (see also Chapter 15) should be to provide the information and forecasts for:

- institutional investors to decide to invest
- the target and maximum purchase prices to be assessed
- the financial structure of the deal to be determined.

The plan should be written by the management team and must provide a comprehensive picture. The corporate finance advisers should provide guidance and review the plan to ensure that it is an effective document to help sell the deal to investors.

Investors do not expect everything to go according to plan, so they expect to see:

- risk areas and uncertainties identified
- plans to address current or potential problems and to minimise their impact
- contingency plans if problems do occur
- sensitivity analysis to answer 'what if' questions.

Content

The plan should include:

- an executive summary
- the company:
  - history
  - present ownership
  - location
  - key products and services
  - suitability for a buy-out or buy-in
  - commercial rationale for making the proposed investment.
- the marketplace, marketing and selling:
  - the size of the marketplace and forecast growth
  - competition and a comparative assessment of products and services in terms of performance and pricing
  - major customers and distributors
  - marketing, selling and sales channels and promotion plans.
- manufacturing and distribution:
  - land and buildings
  - production facilities
  - use of technology
  - surplus capacity
  - need for additional capital investment
  - key suppliers and subcontractors
  - warehousing and distribution.
- technical information:
  - current and proposed R&D projects
  - patents, licences and trade marks
  - anticipated technological developments within the industry and the planned response.
- people
  - members of the buy-out team
  - organisational structure

- other key employees and expertise
- staff relations and any trade union or staff association involvement.
- financial summary:
    - estimated purchase price
    - anticipated time to realise the investment and likely exit routes
    - working capital requirements
    - historical and forecast profit and loss accounts and cash flow figures, covering the next three years
    - budgeting, monthly reporting and financial management procedures.

The appendices should include the following information:

- detailed financial projections of profit and loss and cash flow for the next three years, supported by a statement of all assumptions used and sensitivity analysis
- management biographies:
    - factual biographies of each member of the buy-out or buy-in team and other key managers and staff
    - qualifications, previous employers, positions held and tangible achievements should be detailed; waffle should be avoided.
- published information:
    - product and services brochures
    - press comment and articles.

Negotiating the deal

Key matters to be resolved, in addition to the purchase price, include:

- the use and cost of central services which will be needed for an interim period until alternative facilities are created within the company; for example, access to group information technology resources
- rights to intellectual property, such as patents, trade marks, trading names and licences
- the cost of any redundancies
- the transfer of pension scheme benefits
- the structure of the deal and the tax implications for both parties
- warranties and indemnities.

In most cases, tough and expert negotiation is needed to achieve a satisfactory price for a buy-out or a buy-in. The burden of debt interest means that there is usually a fine dividing line between an acceptable purchase price and one which prohibits a deal altogether.

Staff

Motivation and morale should improve following a management buy-out or buy-in. There is a risk, however, that a 'them or us' attitude could develop, separating the management team that has invested in the business from the remainder of the management and staff.

Serious consideration should be given to creating staff incentive schemes on the completion of the deal. Depending upon current tax regulations, attractive incentive schemes may be provided by:

- profit-sharing
- share options
- saving-based share purchases.

It is nothing less than enlightened self-interest to err on the generous side when creating incentives for management and staff in either an MBO or an MBI deal.

BUSINESS SEMINARS

Focused on developing your potential

Falconbury, the sister company to Thorogood publishing, brings together the leading experts from all areas of management and strategic development to provide you with a comprehensive portfolio of action-centred training and learning.

We understand everything managers and leaders need to **be, know and do** to succeed in today's commercial environment. Each product addresses a different technical or personal development need that will encourage growth and increase your potential for success.

- Practical public training programmes
- Tailored in-company training
- Coaching
- Mentoring
- Topical business seminars
- Trainer bureau/bank
- Adair Leadership Foundation

The most valuable resource in any organisation is its people; it is essential that you invest in the development of your management and leadership skills to ensure your team fulfil their potential. Investment into both personal and professional development has been proven to provide an outstanding ROI through increased productivity in both you and your team. Ultimately leading to a dramatic impact on the bottom line.

With this in mind Falconbury have developed a comprehensive portfolio of training programmes to enable managers of all levels to develop their skills in leadership, communications, finance, people management, change management and all areas vital to achieving success in today's commercial environment.

What Falconbury can offer you?

- Practical applied methodology with a proven results
- Extensive bank of experienced trainers
- Limited attendees to ensure one-to-one guidance
- Up to the minute thinking on management and leadership techniques
- Interactive training
- Balanced mix of theoretical and practical learning
- Learner-centred training
- Excellent cost/quality ratio

Falconbury In-Company Training

Falconbury are aware that a public programme may not be the solution to leadership and management issues arising in your firm. Involving only attendees from your organisation and tailoring the programme to focus on the current challenges you face individually and as a business may be more appropriate. With this in mind we have brought together our most motivated and forward thinking trainers to deliver tailored in-company programmes developed specifically around the needs within your organisation.

All our trainers have a practical commercial background and highly refined people skills. During the course of the programme they act as facilitator, trainer and mentor, adapting their style to ensure that each individual benefits equally from their knowledge to develop new skills.

Falconbury works with each organisation to develop a programme of training that fits your needs.

Mentoring and coaching

Developing and achieving your personal objectives in the workplace is becoming increasingly difficult in today's constantly changing environment. Additionally, as a manager or leader, you are responsible for guiding colleagues towards the realisation of their goals. Sometimes it is easy to lose focus on your short and long-term aims.

Falconbury's one-to-one coaching draws out individual potential by raising self-awareness and understanding, facilitating the learning and performance development that creates excellent managers and leaders. It builds renewed self-confidence and a strong sense of 'can-do' competence, contributing significant benefit to the organisation. Enabling you to focus your energy on developing your potential and that of your colleagues.

Mentoring involves formulating winning strategies, setting goals, monitoring achievements and motivating the whole team whilst achieving a much improved work life balance.

BUSINESS LAW SEMINARS

Falconbury – Business Legal Seminars

Falconbury Business Legal Seminars specialises in the provision of high quality training for legal professionals from both in-house and private practice internationally.

The focus of these events is to provide comprehensive and practical training on current international legal thinking and practice in a clear and informative format.

Event subjects include, drafting commercial agreements, employment law, competition law, intellectual property, managing an in-house legal department and international acquisitions.

For more information on all our services please contact Falconbury on: +44 (0) 20 7729 6677 or visit the website at: www.falconbury.co.uk.